Circus of the
Mind in Motion

CIRCUS

of the

MIND

in

MOTION

Postmodernism
and the
Comic Vision

Lance Olsen

Wayne State University Press
Detroit 1990

Library of Congress Cataloging-in-Publication Data

Olsen, Lance, 1956–
    Circus of the mind in motion : postmodernism and the comic vision /
Lance Olsen.
       p.   cm. — (Humor in life and letters)
    Includes bibliographical references.
    ISBN 0-8143-2132-1
    1. Comic, The, in literature.   2. Postmodernism (Literature)
3. Black humor (Literature)   4. Literature, Modern—20th century—
History and criticism.   I. Title.   II. Series.
PN56.C66047 1990
809'.917—dc20   89-39857
                                                                      CIP

Copyright Acknowledgments

    Part of the argument of Chapter 1 was developed
in an essay that appeared in *Thalia: Studies in Literary Humor* 10.1 (1989) and one that appeared in *Studies in Iconography* 11 (1987), which is reprinted with
the permission of *Studies in Iconography,* School of
Art, Arizona State University.
    An earlier version of Chapter 2 appeared in the
Journal of Narrative Technique 16.2 (1986), reprinted
by permission of the *Journal of Narrative Technique.*
    An earlier version of Chapter 3 appeared in *Mod-
ern Fiction Studies* 32.1 (1986). *Modern Fiction Studies* © 1986 by Purdue Research Foundation, West La-
fayette, Indiana 47907. Reprinted with permission.
    An earlier version of Chapter 5 appeared in *South
Atlantic Review* 51.4 (1986): 69–77, and is reprinted
with the permission of the *South Atlantic Review.*

Andrea

Theory is good, but it doesn't prevent things
from happening.
—Charcot quoted by Freud quoted by
Thomas, *The White Hotel*

Contents

Acknowledgments

George Meredith once said there is nothing like a theory for blinding the wise. The opposite, alas, is also true: there is nothing like the *lack* of a theory for blinding the wise. One tends to miss the forest for the trees or the trees for the forest. And sometimes one misses both at once. To the extent that I have seen anything at all in the following pages, I am indebted to a number of people.

From the bottom of my heart I should like to thank my Postmodern Humor classes at the University of Kentucky (spring 1987 and 1988) who taught me a congress of wonders; my Contemporary Culture class (summer 1988) at King's College, University of London, who taught me that Whitby is a state of mind; my Postmodern Culture class (fall 1987) in the Honors Program at Kentucky, who taught me education will never be the same again.

Many postmodern blessings upon Walter Abish, Guy Davenport, William Gass, Gurney Norman, and Ronald Sukenick, who all graciously endured my questions about their work and about postmodernity; to my very good buddies Patricia Troxel and Arthur Wrobel for their meticulous scrutiny of my prose and thought during the manuscript preparation; to Janet Elred, Joyce and Aaron Garvin, Marcia Hurlow, Violet Olsen, Ellen Rosenman, Janine Scancarelli, John Shawcross, Greg Stump, David Troxel, Jeff and Linda Worley, and David Youngblood, who lent support innumerable ways and taught me more than I can articulate about the nature of friendship; and to the memory of sweet Sheldon, who kept an eye out for me for years and taught me again and again that real existence could be radically comic.

Last and most, widest and deepest, all my love and gratitude to Andrea, my existential cohort, my Hardy and my Costello, for things too numerous and important to mention here.

I
THE
TIGHTROPE

1.

Toward a Theory of Postmodern Humor, or: Christa McAuliffe and the Banana Peel

My nourishment is refined from the ongoing circus of the mind in motion. Give me the odd linguistic trip, stutter and fall, and I will be content.
—Donald Barthelme, *Snow White*

The Emblem

I heard this joke within forty-eight hours of the space shuttle Challenger turning into a fireball before several million viewers in 1986 and killing all seven crew members on board, including a schoolteacher.

> QUESTION: What was the last thing to go through Christa McAuliffe's mind?
> ANSWER: Her asshole.

Here, There, and Everywhere

Now we could try to pass that off as just an aberration, some misfire of taste. Or we could become dismayed, grouchy, even disgusted by such inhumane and harmful joking. But I'm not sure we

15

would be completely honest with ourselves if we did. Certainly, we wouldn't be true to our contemporary experience, since such joking has become more and more typical these days.

Surely what I shall call postmodern humor has always been around to one degree or another. It is, as I hope will become clear, less a chronological fact than a state of mind that surfaces at various times and in various places—wacky graffiti on the walls of Rome, dark jokes in English monasteries. That is not my point. My point is its profusion now. My point is its easy access to the media of the dominant culture, a proliferation and intensity that would have been unheard of in, say, first-century Rome or tenth-century England.

Monty Python's *Holy Grail* gives us a gruesomely funny image of the terrible black knight, always ready to fight, having his arms and legs whacked away by his opponent. When he is nothing but a blood-spurting human trunk, he shouts at his departing attacker: "Come back here and I'll bite your kneecap off!" Blanche Knott cranks out anthologies called *Truly Tasteless Jokes* with sections on, among other topics, dead babies, Helen Keller, cruelty to animals, and the handicapped.

But we cannot take solace that such joking is solely the product of our popular culture, an anti-intellectual preterite, and thereby dismiss the jokes and the preterite as merely vulgar and lowbrow. After all, Nobel Laureate Samuel Beckett writes of an elderly legless husband and wife who live in ash bins lined with sawdust and who come out only long enough to check whether it is time yet for love—though, alas, they wouldn't know exactly what to do if it were. Poor Nagg has lost a tooth and poor Nell is almost blind, but Nagg at least discovers momentary comfort in the realization that the couple's hearing hasn't failed them. "Our what?" Nell asks (*Endgame* 15). In *Breakfast of Champions* Kurt Vonnegut, "to give an idea of the maturity of [his] illustrations for this book" (5), draws a picture of a human anus, a beaver next to a woman's pubic area, and female underpants. Thomas Pynchon in *V.* describes a woman named Esther being given a nose job by a sadistic doctor named Schoenmaker and his assistant Trench who, during a series of injections to Esther's septum, doesn't miss the sexual metaphor at work. While the doctor shoots, Trench chants: "Stick it in . . . pull it out . . . stick it in . . . ooh that was good . . . pull it out . . ." (92). And there is always the (in)famous scene in *Gravity's Rainbow* when Tyrone Slothrop squirms down a toilet bowl in the men's room at the Roseland Ballroom in pursuit of his fallen mouth harp and finds himself caught in a "murky shitstorm"

(66) with a "Negro dingleberry" stuck up his nose, "stubborn as a wintertime booger as he probes for it" (67).

Nor can we take solace that such jokes are solely the product of a so-called literary establishment—or antiestablishment. Andy Warhol in 1964 began to delight in car accidents and electric chairs and decided to make them part of his Disaster Series. In *Lavender Disaster* he repeats the image of an empty electric chair fifteen times in five rows of three photos each. Henry Cowell, who taught George Gershwin and John Cage at Columbia University between 1951 and 1965, perverted a Keystone Kops skit by crawling inside pianos on stage and plucking their strings like those of a harp. In 1961 Luciano Berio composed *Visage*, a tribute to the radio. It is twenty-one minutes and four seconds of Cathy Berberian's voice laughing, crying, orgasming, singing, echoing patterns of inflections modeled on specific languages, all the while trying but virtually failing to produce articulate speech. She *virtually* fails because in fact one word *is* finally pronounced. The word, ironically and paradoxically, is *parole*, the Italian word for *word*.

The De(con)structive Impulse

At the very moment modernism came to the fore in our culture and dedicated itself to a monumental and relentless humorlessness in the projects of such creators as Mies van der Rohe, Kasimir Malevich, and Rainer Maria Rilke, postmoderns such as Duchamp and the other Dadaists were busy attending performances of Alfred Jarry's protoabsurdist *Ubu Roi* and Raymond Roussel's *Impressions of Africa*. While British troops fought the Third Battle of Ypres, losing four hundred thousand men and gaining five miles of territory over five months of violence, Duchamp tried to exhibit a white procelain urinal with the name *R. Mutt*—a pun on the German word *Armut* ("poverty"), an allusion to "poor man's" art—scrawled on its edge.

About the time the representatives of the victorious countries gathered at Versailles and other Parisian suburbs, Duchamp penciled in a goatee on a reproduction of the *Mona Lisa*. He wasn't merely one of the avant-garde pushing the boundaries of painting and sculpture,

17

posing ever more fundamental aesthetic questions. He was also directly attacking a center of power by means of a special brand of humor that was not just fancy satire wielded against a subject to diminish it in order ultimately to improve it. Duchamp had no intention of improving or even changing the critics' minds. Rather, his impulse was to subvert a power structure for no other reason than the pleasure of subverting a power structure.

From this perspective, Duchamp's humor—quintessentially postmodern in nature—has much to do with Mack Sennett's definition of comedy in general: "whaling the daylights out of Pretension or Authority," thereby posing "the question 'Is nothing sacred?' and [answering] with a fart" (quoted by Charney 246). That is, the impetus of postmodern humor is to disarm pomposity and power. The postmodern creator becomes aesthetic and metaphysical terrorist, a freeplayer in a universe of intertextuality where no one text has any more or less authority than any other.

In a way, then, such joking shares much with absurdist black humor. It is charged with a bitterness and cynicism in the face of a world it perceives as undergoing physical and metaphysical erasure. Its irony is acidic, biting, and, to use Wayne Booth's term, unstable. The audience often senses a complexity and subtlety of tone, but because the postmodern creator manipulates a system of private instead of public norms, his or her final position remains uncertain. He or she "refuses to declare him[/her]self, however subtly, *for* any stable proposition" (Booth 240). Because of this, his or her text exists to be interpreted in radically different, even contradictory, ways.

Witness, for instance, the critical industry that has grown up around Beckett's work. It, we are told, is at once Christian and humanist in nature: obsessed as it is by man's relationship with God and believing the world devoid of all meaning save that which man gives it. It is deeply Freudian and antipsychological. It is firmly set in Ireland and France and abstractly set outside political and geographical reality. It is comic and tragic. It is existentialist, stoic, and nihilist—all at once. After the performance of Beckett's first play, *Le Kid,* a 1931 juvenile parody of Corneille's *Cid* and nod to Charlie Chaplin's *The Kid,* the Trinity College newspaper lampooned the production saying: "I wish [Beckett] would explain his explanations" (Cohn viii). Beckett's audience has continually attempted imposing explanations on works which themselves seek to overturn explanation. Godot, for example, has become "God, a diminutive god, Love, Death, Silence, Hope, De Gaulle, a Balzac character, a bicycle racer, Time Future, and a Paris street for call girls" (Cohn 64)—all in spite of or perhaps *because* of the fact that Beckett himself has stated that his "work is a matter of fundamental sounds . . . and [he] accept[s] responsibility for nothing else. If people want to have headaches among the overtones, let them. And provide their own aspirin" (Bair 470). Beckett in particular—and postmodernism in general—has transformed interpretation into a study of reader-responses. Postmodernism creates texts such as those found in Jorge Luis Borges's fantastic land of Tlön where every book "invariably include[s] thesis and antithesis, the strict pro and con of a theory. A book which does not include its opposite, or 'counter-book,' is considered incomplete" (29).

However, there is more than destructive absurdist black humor at work in the postmodern enterprise. Black humor's thrust is a nihilistic one. If we ask an undergraduate, we will be told that postmodernity adds up to a depressing Nothing, that its goal is to decompose and dismember. Alongside this essentially easy and negative reading, though, exists a more positive one. Beside postmodern humor's dark impetus exists an essentially light impetus. After all, absences may signal emptiness and the lack of meaning, but they also signal gaps that need to be filled and that can be filled in an infinity of ways. In other words, while they may signal the possibility of *de*struction, they also signal the possibility for *con*struction, a radical freedom, a renewed sense of potential. The recognition of the presence of exhaustion is, as John Barth has demonstrated, a prerequisite for replenishment. What is striking about postmodern humor, then, is its refusal to see truth as something that exists along an either-or axis. Consequently, postmodern humor at the same time becomes *both* a negative *and* a positive perspective on the world. It simultaneously holds within itself the destructive and nihilistic force of absurdist black humor (Duchamp gratuitously defaces and delegitimates a "masterpiece" by Leonardo) and the constructive and affirmative force of creative freeplay (Duchamp revels in such an imaginative and ultimately weightless act). Postmodern humor delights in its own sense of liberty. It delights in its own sense of process. Indeed, process is everything because the goal is at best uncertain, at worst nonexistent.

Pynchon's Herbert Stencil comes to understand that what is important about his quest for V. is his *quest* for V.: "if he should find her, where else would there be to go but back into half-consciousness? He tried not to think, therefore, about any end to the search. Approach and avoid" (44). Enzian in *Gravity's Rainbow* knows that "the search will rule" (525). Moreover, the end to pure process can be disasterous. As a warning, Pynchon tells the joke about the boy born with

19

a golden screw where his navel should have been. He spends much of his life roaming the world and talking to specialists, trying to find someone who will help him. He finally comes across a voodoo doctor who gives him a potion that sends him into a wild dream. When he wakes up the golden screw is gone. In ecstasy that his quest is finally over, the boy jumps out of bed and his ass falls off (*V.* 30).

Microhumor: Explaining the Joke

To recap: postmodern humor is an attitude that has arisen at various times in various places but which has gained a striking prominence in our contemporary culture both in "high" and "low" art—if, in fact, such a distinction can still be made. Moreover, it does not simply represent a destructive or constructive thrust, but, paradoxically, both at once.

Now it is time to back up and begin again, taking the key terms of the above assertion and examining each more closely. To do so, let us return for a moment to the McAuliffe joke and ask: What's so funny about such a seemingly awful thing? How does it—and, by implication, most jokes, postmodern or otherwise—work? And, perhaps more interesting, why do many people who even acknowledge its bad taste laugh at it? Following D. H. Monro's helpful classification in his piece, "Humor," I should like to suggest that theorists offer answers along one of three definitional routes: humor as an appeal to superiority, to relief from restraint, or to incongruity.

When we hear the Christa McAuliffe joke within forty-eight hours of the space shuttle disaster, some deep part of us secretly feels relieved that the accident didn't happen to us, that we got by this time. We are alive and Christa McAuliffe is dead. For a moment, we actually find ourselves taking a certain degree of pleasure in the misfortune of another. We feel, however fleetingly, superior to the schoolteacher. This kind of logic—which strikes many of us intuitively and painfully close to home—has its foundations in Thomas Hobbes's notion that laughter stems from a sudden sense of eminency over the infirmities of others or over the infirmities of ourselves at an earlier time. In *The Emotions and the Will,* Alexander Bain reinforces Hobbes's observation by suggesting that laughter arises when we "plunge the venerated object into a degrading conjunction" (284). Henri Bergson in "Laughter" indicates that what sparks our impulse to degrade is the perception of "something mechanical encrusted on the living" (84), the inability of something or someone to adapt to a continually mutable environment.

Another way to begin to account for what happens to us when we hear the McAuliffe joke is to think about the pain, anger, and frustration we all felt when we first heard about the disaster. Our culture only allows us to exhibit such emotions briefly and ritualistically and then all is back to business as usual. Initially, the spectators were speechless. Later in the day President Reagan appeared on national television to comfort the people of the United States by framing the disaster in a set of elegiac conventions. Later still, *Wheel of Fortune* went on without a hitch, as though everything were just as it should be. Nonetheless, our pain, anger, and frustration did not disappear. Rather, our culture told us to repress the emotions so that we could continue to function normally. At the moment we heard the joke, though, we understood unconsciously that decorum had been trespassed and that we were allowed a brief emotional release from cultural restraint. And we laughed.

Immanuel Kant argues along these lines in *Critique of Judgement* when he writes that laughter arises from "a rapidly alternating tension and relaxation" that effects "a motion conducive to health" (179), as does Bain in "Wit and Humour" when he says that "we are agreeably relieved by laughter, which is a convulsive tottering and relapse from the high and dignified to the vulgar and easy" (37). But it is Sigmund Freud who is most commonly associated with this approach. In *Wit and Its Relation to the Unconscious* he asserts that "the conditions for laughter are such that a sum of psychic energy hitherto employed in the cathexis of some paths may experience free discharge" (734). Laughter, then, momentarily frees up a forbidden idea or emotion.

A third way to account for our laughter when we hear the McAuliffe joke has to do with the incongruity between what we expect and what we receive. When someone asks us "What was the last thing to go through Christa McAuliffe's mind?," we assume, because of the grammatical structure of the question and because of similar questions we have heard in the past, that the sentence means "What was Christa McAuliffe's last thought?" As a result, we cue into a grid of possible answers, all having to do with mental processes, perhaps certain revelations. We fail to see the ambiguity present in the question. So when we are told the answer is "Her asshole," we metaphorically trip over our own feet, the ideal is undercut by the real, and we become as much the target of the joke as does Christa McAuliffe. As Kant has it, we experience "the sudden transformation of a strained expectation into nothing" (177). In *The World as Will*

21

and Representation Arthur Schopenhauer makes essentially the same point when he discovers that at the core of much joking lies a syllogism with an accepted major premise and an unexpected and unsound minor one.

Obviously, each of these approaches is limited in one way or another. Or, more precisely, each understands humor at a different level and dimension, thereby leaving out a number of other levels and dimensions. Superiority theory sees humor as a struggle for power and control, as primarily aggressive. Indeed, this accounts for much humor, particularly for postmodernity's subset of absurdist black humor. But it doesn't account for essentially good-spirited humor fairly unconcerned with power relations. Relief theory, on the other hand, sees humor's psychological and sociological dimensions, usually attempting to explain what both the individual and his or her society must repress in order to remain sane. But even Freud saw that not all humor was tied to a release of aggressive or sexual inhibitions. Beside this kind of humor, he argued, lies harmless wit that is indulged in for its own sake. Both superiority theory and relief theory are concerned with the content of humor. Neither takes into account humor's form. This is where incongruity theory comes in. Incongruity theory may be seen as a structural approach to humor, reducing humor as it does to its quintessential formula. While it accounts for a wealth of both good- and mean-spirited humor, incongruity theory fails to account for the emotional how's and why's.

All three theories also tend to be long on explanations concerning specific jokes and specific laughter-generating situations and short on general accounts of the nature of the comic vision. Here it is necessary to pull back from individual theories attempting to explicate individual jokes and ask: Exactly what do all these theories add up to? If we move from microhumor (the joke, the text of a sentence or paragraph, for instance), to macrohumor (the comic vision, the text of a whole novel or play), what do we find? What are the attitudes and values of comedy—all comedy, not just the postmodern version—as a whole?

Macrohumor: From Joke to Comic Vision

Don E. Elgin primarily emphasizes the positive values in comedy when he embraces an "ecological esthetics" (222). Basing his theory on that of Joseph Meeker in *Comedy of Survival,* Elgin asserts that much of Western culture has so far reinforced a tragic vision of reality by reminding man that he is noble and spiritual—and thereby separating him from the universe around him. Tragedy privileges man's interest in man while devaluing man's interest in his environment. Moreover, tragedy places man above his environment. Comedy—which since Aristotle's *Poetics* has received much less critical attention than the tragic—does the opposite. The comic vision "springs from [man's] conviction that he is a part of the [eco]system and that, unless the [eco]system exists, he has little chance of doing so himself" (Elgin 223). The comic vision reinforces man's role as survivor and man's infinitely complex interconnection with life itself. Man is joined with his environment "physically, morally, and intellectually," and he must continually "adapt himself to the complex natural system" (224). Man is not *above* nature in the comic view. Rather, he must be at one with it in order to survive. Although Elgin mentions in passing a model balance between creative and destuctive forces in comedy, he in fact bases his argument on the former to the near exclusion of the latter.

Closer to the mark is Edward L. Galligan's view. He asserts that Western culture is the only one to have developed a tragic vision of life, which has been expressed "in only a small number of works created in a few periods of history," whereas the comic vision "is ubiquitous; all major and most minor [cultures] have developed a comic vision and expressed it in diverse works in every form known to the imagination" (23). Grounding his argument on that in William Lynch's *Christ and Apollo*, Galligan claims that the tragic mode ultimately speaks of human defeat, whereas the comic mode shows man as unbreakable. The tragic vision deals only with part of the life cycle, whereas the comic vision deals with the whole. The tragic vision teaches us about despair and death, whereas the comic vision teaches us about hope and life. Moreover, the comic vision teaches us that despair is a simplistic and cowardly vision, that "actually it is hopefulness that calls for inconvenient kinds and quantities of courage; it requires first that we search what is out there to find if there is some way or place we may thrive, and then that we change, or at least abandon our pretensions, in order to fit into that place" (29).

At the core of the comic vision, Galligan intimates, is a subversive impulse directed toward the dominant culture. The comic vision sees life not as work but festival, not as Puritan hardship but as playful pastime. The comic protagonist is always less concerned with mastering his environment than with making sure his environment doesn't master him. The comic vision loves to pull the rug out from under wishful thinking, egocentricism, affected dignity, silly pedantry, absurd pride, willfulness, and other human follies. Indeed, the comic protagonist often finds himself pulling the rug out from under his own feet, making himself the brunt of his own jokes, which makes the comic particularly hard on everyone—including its audience—since its message is that man is less noble than he is a numbskull. And finally the comic derides any univocal vision. It attacks the inability to see several perspectives simultaneously. It calls for "acute double [or I would argue more accurately *multiple*] vision in contradictory circumstances, which are the circumstances most of us live in" (34). Consequently, and perhaps paradoxically, the comic vision accepts injustice and therefore the destructive as part of the world and as the price of life.

At the end of Joseph Heller's *Catch-22,* just when it seems there is no more hope to be had, we learn that Orr has rowed for weeks and weeks in his little yellow raft with his tiny blue paddle, eating raw codfish and drinking tea, and has finally reached Sweden. "It's a miracle of human perseverance," the chaplain says. "I'm going to run away," Yossarian says. "You can't run away," Major Danby says. "Where can you run to? Where can you go?" Yossarian tells the major he can go to Sweden, and Danby insists the move is dangerous, naive, cowardly, and irresponsible. Yossarian laughs at him, at how easily Danby buys into the system bent on killing him. "I'm not running *away* from my responsibilities, "Yossarian tells Danby. "I'm running *to* them. There's nothing negative about running away to save my life" (458–63). Yossarian jumps out the window, and Nately's whore, who has been waiting for him, tries to stab him. She misses, though, and Yossarian is gone. Nately's whore will follow him forever, a universal principle in the landscape reminding him he must always be on his toes, that not all play is safe, that adapting to one's environment isn't always easy, and that, as Yogi Berra once said, the game isn't over till it's over. But Yossarian is going to live forever, or die trying. And *that* is the comic vision.

The *P* Word as a State of Mind

As Allen Thiher and I have suggested before, it is less important whether or not postmodernism in fact exists (in what way, after all, can romanticism or Victorianism be said to exist save as a shorthand for a series of more or less shared concerns and techniques?) than whether or not we as a culture feel the need to *assert* that postmodernism exists. Whether or not in two years or ten or a hundred some theorist sits down and decides to call everything written after Descartes the Age of Selfhood or the Age of Uncertainty or the Age of the Cogito is, obviously, of little interest to us here and now, as we slowly brace ourselves and our culture for a new *fin de siècle*. What *is* of interest is that, as Umberto Eco proposes, we view ourselves as living in a between-times, a "new Middle Ages" (488) where "a great Peace . . . is breaking down, [and] a great international state power that had unified the world in language, customs, ideologies, religion, art and technology . . . [is] collaps[ing]"(490).

And what *should be* of much interest to us all is that on 22 June 1986, the *New York Times Book Review* ran a front-page essay by Denis Donoghue called "The Promiscuous Cool of Postmodernism." What is dazzling about this event is that one of the most popular newspapers of the literary establishment decided to say it too had seen the unicorn and had decided to pass on the Word to its general readership. Granted, Donoghue's tone is often cranky ("I thought we had finished with these matters, but I see they are still on every academic agenda," he begins [1]) and he adds nothing new by way of insight or definition ("The art of postmodernism is chiefly characterized by the elegance of its pastiche," he claims [37], simply and incompletely echoing one of the central ideas in Fredric Jameson's seminal 1982 essay, "Postmodernism and Consumer Society"). Nonetheless, with the appearance of his essay the culture at large suddenly acknowledged, if not wholly endorsed, the concept of the postmodern. Suddenly, a group of academics no longer must apologize when they use the term. They no longer need to articulate the predictable statements concerning the term's ugliness, vagueness, or hipness. Moreover, the term has appeared with greater and greater frequency over the last few years in magazines as diverse as *Salmagundi* and *The Atlantic*. And the *MLA Directory of Periodicals* even acknowledges the presence of *Boundary 2: A Journal of Postmodern Literature and Culture* and lists its 1987 circulation at 1,250. That is to say, the unicorn has found a nest—if that is what unicorns find—and has settled down to stay, at least for a while.

What is also dazzling about the appearance of Donoghue's piece is that it is as much a register of an omega as of an alpha. To bring the avant-garde into the establishment is to begin to traditionalize the avant-garde, to stabilize a way of thinking whose essence is destabilization. As soon as we have agreed upon a term, a menu, a system of conventions for the postmodern—and it appears that in some ways as a culture we already have or are, at least, well on our way to doing so—petrifaction has begun. Something has, as Beckett's Clov knows, run its course. As Walter Abish said recently when I asked him if he still placed himself in the company of the postmoderns: "What is postmodern anymore? What is experimental? The word has lost its meaning. Do people read Robbe-Grillet as an experimental writer these days? Certainly not." After such an observation, it is only a matter of time before our incredibly self-conscious culture attempts to define itself once again, and once again differently. After all, several generations of thinkers and creators have grown up postmodern. It cannot be long before the postmodern begins to resemble the norm.

My own petrifaction of postmodernism underscores that the post-modern is less a historical period than a mode of consciousness; it has less to do with chronology than it does with perspective. While it has come to dominance since the Second World War, one can hear post-modern atonality and hyper–self-reflexivity in works by writers as varied as Miguel de Cervantes, Laurence Sterne, Herman Melville, and Franz Kafka. Whereas modern consciousness developed a number of responses to the situation in which it found itself—responses that created a sense of underlying coherence and order, as in the mythological structures informing *The Waste Land, Ulysses,* and *As I Lay Dying*—postmodern consciousness can no longer find a response adequate to the situation in which it finds itself. It concerns itself, as Jean-François Lyotard indicates, with presenting the unpresentable. Fredric Jameson and Jean Baudrillard find schizophrenia as the appro-priate psychological analogue for this state. For Baudrillard "the schizo is bereft of every scene, open to everything in spite of himself, living in the greatest confusion. . . . He can no longer produce the limits of his own being, can no longer play nor stage himself, can no longer produce himself as mirror" (133).

The postmodern has deconstructed the notion of the transcenden-tal signified and hence turned the universe—to use Roland Barthes's terms—from a *work* into a *text.* "We know now," Barthes asserts, "that a text is not a line of words releasing a single 'theological' meaning (the 'message' of the Author-God) but a multidimensional space in which a variety of writings, none of them original, blend and clash" (146). When the Author-God has been removed from the text—and we must remember that for the postmoderns the world and the self are texts—all limits on the text are abandoned. When all limits are abandoned, the text ceases to possess one and only one meaning. The textual universe opens into multiplicity. Postmodernism thereby "liberates what may be called an anti-theological activity, an activity that is truly revolutionary since to refuse to fix meaning is, in the end, to refuse God and his hypostases—reason, science, law" (147).

In *The Postmodern Condition* Lyotard essentially expands on Barthes's reading by suggesting that while modern and premodern consciousnesses appeal to the idea of a metanarrative—an overarching narrative that tells The Story about knowledge and culture—postmodern consciousness expresses incredulity toward metanarratives. To phrase matters slightly more rigorously, I should like to suggest that, while each premodern consciousness *believed* in a metanarrative (God in the Middle Ages, Man in the Renaissance, Reason in Neoclassicism, and so on), modern consciousness *sought to believe* in a metanarrative (Yeats's quest for a private mythology, Eliot's search for the Tradition, Hemingway's longing for the Code) and postmodern consciousness basks in the proliferation of micronarratives. In *Just Gaming* Lyotard asserts that the result of this approach is, or at least should be, a plethora of language games, none of which is privileged over any other; each game could be changed as the mood or need arises.

As Alan Wilde argues, then, the dominant postmodern response is acceptance: my answer or lack of answer is as valid or invalid as your answer or lack of answer. In a pluriverse of intertextuality and plurisignification, postmodernism delights in detotalizing univocality. It thereby delights in antiform, chance, dispersal, misreading, and uncertainty. If, as Andreas Huyssen maintains, modern consciousness constitutes itself through "a strategy of exclusion" that insists on an "obsessive hostility to mass culture" and a "programmatic distance from political, economic, and social concerns" (vii), then postmodern consciousness breaks down all boundaries between high and low culture and explores—sometimes even embraces—political, economic, and social concerns.

Postmodernity, then, is a radically skeptical state of mind whose impulse is to decenter, detotalize, and deconstruct while taking nothing—including its own (non)premises—very seriously.

The Death of Intelligent Writing

This is obviously not to suggest that postmodernism is the *only* mode of consciousness or expression extant in the second half of the twentieth century. Since the early 1970s, for example, there has been a revitalization of realism as a narrative mode via such writers as

27

James Alan McPherson, Jayne Anne Phillips, Bobbie Ann Mason, and Raymond Carver. Such a conservative narrative strategy indicates a conservative metaphysical strategy. It believes in a world out there, an empirical world that the reader can smell, see, and touch. It believes in logic, chronology, and plot. It believes in stable identity, in a sense of self, in depth psychology. It believes in a universe of communal reality and common sense, where content is privileged over form, language is transparent, style is secondary, and, it is assumed, the word mirrors the world.

This neorealism expresses, as Mas'ud Zavarzadeh and many other experimentalists have affirmed, a nostalgia for the old realism. It expresses a nostalgia for the empiricism and pragmatism of the nineteenth century and the early part of our own, for the prose and metaphysics of Flaubert, Tolstoy, even Dreiser. Consequently, it is in the purest sense a conservative vision of reality—a vision, that is, that wishes to *conserve* a way of writing, a way of seeing, a moral and humanist optic through which one looks backwards rather than ahead. T. C. Boyle calls it Catatonic Realism. Richard Kostelanetz calls it the death of intelligent writing. Larry McCaffery calls it the Walden Book Syndrome and attributes it to the gobbling up of smaller publishers by multinational corporations that encourage stocking only books that are bound to make a big buck. I attribute it to the Age of Kohl-Thatcher-Reagan and the growing neoconservative political attacks on the culture and ideals of the 1960s.

The advent of such neoconservatism has prompted several critics to sound the death knell of pure postmodernity—rightly, I am coming to believe. In his important essay, "Mapping the Postmodern," Huyssen traces several generations of postmodernism and points to current attempts to restore a 1950s version of high modernism for the 1980s. Ihab Hassan in *The Postmodern Turn* discerns three distinct phases of postmodernism. The first, which grew directly out of modernism's "multitemporal and fragmentary awareness," displays "a cool, diffuse avant-gardis[m]." The second displays a "reflexive, parodic bent," which is manifested in the metafictionalists. The third, which appeared during the late 1970s, is a phase of dispersal where postmodernism fractured "into various eclectic tendencies: some—in music, art, and architecture—neoromantic, others kitsch, camp, pop, deconstructionist, neodadist, hermetically reflexive, or simply otiose" (216).

Such phases strike me as a bit too tidy, but I do sense a general arc in postmodernism's life—from an outgrowth of modernism in the late forties and fifties (Borges, Nabokov, and Burgess) to an apex of purified formlessness in the late fifties, sixties, and early seventies (Beckett, Pynchon, and Sorrentino) to a faded form in the late seventies and eighties that has begun to merge again with modernism and even realism (William Kennedy, Don DeLillo, and Raymond Carver—and, in the art world, Neoexpressionism).

Postmodernism's demise—or, more precisely, its movement from dominant to recessive cultural trait—raises a series of questions: How long can we live as true postmoderns? How long can we exist—both textually, and, more basically, in the nitty-gritty and derrière-garde day-to-day world of committee meetings, raising children, and political action—in a state analogous to schizophrenia? Or, as Abish implies, how long does the experimental actually remain experimental, the subversive actually subversive, before we simply become accustomed to a certain level of shock, a certain system of "nonconventional" conventions? Certainly, Robbe-Grillet's *Jealousy* jars upon first reading, but what about the second, the third? And what about a generation of readers raised on the very conventions designed to undercut traditional conventions? After we have gutted the world, the self, and language, and hollowed out the core of Western culture, then what? What do we put in place of the rubble, or is our job really to bulldoze relentlessly and forever, like those children in Barthelme's *The Dead Father*? As Hassan writes: "But have we had enough? *That* question, suggesting supervention, *dépassement,* may not be postmodern. Nonetheless, the mere fact that we ask it betrays our impatience, our need for some larger sense of the moment" (*The Postmodern Turn,* 214). Hassan offers in its place—á la Richard Rorty—a personalized version of Jamesian pragmatism. Such a move probably tells us more about Hassan than about our culture in the final analysis, but its very existence is indicative of a larger turn away from postmodern consciousness.

Postmodernism and the Comic Vision

I do not want to intimate, as Julia Kristeva does, that the modern essentially focuses on "the malady of pain" whereas "the postmodern lies closer to the human comedy than to abyssal malaise" (151). It seems to me too simplistic an opposition to say that the modern is somehow fundamentally tragic and the postmodern fundamentally comic. After all, in the midst of Mann and Lawrence there is Joyce and Breton. Nor is postmodernity necessarily comic; in *Ellipse of Uncertainty* I zero in, for the most part, on the "abyssal" side of the postmodern in works by writers such as Alain Robbe-Grillet, Carlos Fuentes, and J. M. Coetzee.

Closer to the mark is the distinction Candace Lang makes between irony and humor. Irony is a state of mind that assumes the presence of a meaning behind or under a given text. In other words, truth is envisioned as the gold that can and should be mined. Such a vision goes back at least as far as Plato, who suggests that a "truer" reality exists behind this one. Humor, on the other hand, is a state of mind that believes primarily in surface, in no positive content. In other words, there is no "truth" to humor, rather, an incessant questioning that yields no ultimate answer. Such a vision goes back at least as far as Socrates whose thought, as Kierkegaard points out, is "not subject to interpretation, in the traditional sense, since there is no underlying message" (Lang 3). The modern text is primarily ironic, for it believes that its intent is to communicate a message (although it chooses to do so in a less "sincere" or direct way than a premodern nonironic text). The postmodern text is primarily humorous; it believes its intent is inconclusive, polyvalent, and unreadable through an ironic optic because there is no meaning tucked under its surface. The humorous, which needn't necessarily be funny, delights in discontinuity; the ironic, which needn't necessarily be sad, mourns it.

At one notorious point in *Gravity's Rainbow*, Säure and Gustav argue over who is better, Rossini or Beethoven. Rossini, we learn, produces "some medley of predictable little tunes," which is "as shameless as eating a whole jar of peanut butter at one sitting" (441). He represents the traditionalist, the conservative, the univocal. Beethoven, on the other hand, represents "the incorporation of more and more notes into the scale, culminating with dodecaphonic democracy, where all notes get an equal hearing"; he represents that which precedes Anton Webern, who rejoices in music's "polymorphous perversity" and who is "the moment of maximum freedom" (440–41). Here, Beethoven represents the prototype of postmodern consciousness. He is an analogue for the Zone in which, as Geli tells Slothrop, one must "forget frontiers now. Forget subdivisions. There aren't any . . . It's all been suspended. Vaslav calls it an 'interregnum.' You only have to flow along with it" (294). It is in the Zone, as Squalidozzi points out, that "our hope is limitless. . . . So is our danger" (265).

Another way of explaining this concept is by employing Mikhail Bakhtin's well-known notion of polyphonics. In his *Problems of Dostoevsky's Poetics,* he claims there are two visions of the world. The first, expressed for example in the novels of Tolstoy, is monologic. No matter how many voices speak in a work of this kind, they are subordinated to the author's univocal sense of truth. The second, expressed for example in the novels of Dostoevsky, is dialogic—or, more accurately, polyphonic. Here voices—each representing a unique point of view—are allowed to speak for themselves. No attempt is made at univocal truth. Rather, every attempt is made to let idea clash with idea. Bakhtin states that an idea truly "begins to live, that is, to take shape, to develop, to find and renew its verbal expression, to give birth to new ideas, only when it enters into genuine dialogic relationships with other ideas, with the ideas of others" (88). The power of polyphonics is that it forces ideas "to quarrel" and it generates "new linkages of ideas . . . new voice-ideas and changes in the arrangement of all the voice-ideas in the worldwide dialogue" (91).

Bakhtin finds the roots of polyphony in the carnival and "carnivalized" genres such as Menippean satire, a heterogeneous mode of discourse composed of mixed prose forms interspersed with verse that foregrounds dialogues among various mental attitudes while backgrounding traditional concerns of character and plot. Northrop Frye calls such a structure an "encyclopaedic farrago" (311), and Brian McHale calls it a "stylistic heteroglossia" (172). Clearly, the comic postmodern, who romps in polyphony, in plurality, in maximum freedom, in a joyous relativity where all that is rigid is overturned, is a descendant of such a mode—not simply an extension, however, but a radical intensification. Indeed, as if to underscore the point, images of carnivals pervade the comic postmodern text, from the weird winding hallways of Borges's fiction to the funhouse in Barth's famous creation, from the Schweinheldfest in *Gravity's Rainbow* to the grotesque country fairs in Ed McClanahan's work.

Richard Keller Simon therefore finds the labyrinth the appropriate metaphor for the comic, since it both indicates the comic's "complexity and confusion" and the idea of "the maze crafted for the king of Crete—symmetrical, dangerous, captivating—in which lurks the monster of mockery that destroys all those who come after it" (8). Perhaps an even more appropriate metaphor for postmodern humor is the one Barthelme creates and the one with which I began this chapter: the circus of the mind in motion. Because both the comic and the postmodern attempt to subvert all centers of authority—including their own—and because they both ultimately deride univocal visions, toppling bigots, cranks, and pompous idiots as they go, they tend to complement each other well. Both seek through radical incongruity of form to short-circuit the dominant culture's repressive impulses. Hence, both are simultaneously destructive and constructive. Both represent a survivalist aesthetics in which, as Edgar, the teacher in Barthelme's story,

31

"The School," knows, it isn't death that gives meaning to life, but "life . . . which gives meaning to life" (311). Both focus on process rather than conclusion. Both embrace plurality, an abundance of language games, and the idea that the universe is a text that may be rewritten in a host of equally acceptable ways. And both therefore understand, along with Johan Huizinga, that "pure play is one of the main bases of civilization" (5). When wedded, postmodernism and comic vision become a *mindcircus* with an infinite number of rings all astir, all swir!ing with wild hoopla, all gorgeous and astonishing. Hierarchies are toppled, and pedants become fools, and fantasy becomes fact, and the sacred becomes wonderfully marvelously profane, and every voice is a dodecaphonic symphony.

In this circus, architect Frank Gehry can make buildings shaped like huge milk jugs. Best Products Company, based in Richmond, Virginia, can commission Hardy Holzman Pfeifer Associates of New York City to design a new headquarters office building that, as Holzman said, looks like a museum one works in; it comes with a medieval moat, several Italian Renaissance fountains, sixteenth-century patterning on the Art Deco glass block façade, and nineteenth-century colonial furniture, and in front of it all sit two titanic eagles that look like enormous bookstands. The Eurythmics can produce a video in which a large cow strolls through a walnut-panelled boardroom while a woman with orange hair sits at a mahogany table playing a home computer like a piano. Roy Lichtenstein can faithfully reproduce comic strips in oil and acrylic and raise them to the level of Art while at the same time deflating paintings by Picasso, Mondrian, Matisse, and other moderns by translating them into his characteristic dot-and-line techniques. Claes Oldenburg can create a sculpture called *Soft Toilet* out of vinyl, plexiglass, and kapok. And in 1961 Piero Manzoni can fill ninety tin cans with his feces and sell them at the going price of gold. Behind each creation lies the shadow of Marcel Duchamp, the man who wanted to use a Rembrandt painting as an ironing board.

There Is Nothing Like a Theory for Blinding the Wise

Critics studying postmodernism or comedy sail a perilous course between a grumpy Scylla and downright nasty Charybdis. They run the risk, on the one hand, of defining themselves right out of a job by being so meticulous and exclusive that they end up, like Elder Olson in *The Theory of Comedy,* having to argue only five of Shakespeare's plays qualify as true comedies—an assertion that strikes just about everyone save the most diehard academic as marvelously inaccurate. On the other hand, they run the risk of creating a loose baggy monster that gobbles up everything in its path, so they end up, like Northrop Frye in *Anatomy of Criticism,* with a small fistful of myths that seem to apply to just about anything—an outcome that is nice and often helpful in a very general way but fails to make particularly subtle distinctions between one artifact and another. In this study, I have decided to run the risk of taking the loose-baggy-monster-that-eats-almost-everything-in-its-path approach. In good keeping with postmodern comedy, I will surely become the brunt of my own joke.

Now such a move needn't necessarily be a bad one as long as we keep several caveats in mind along the way. First, criticism is a process of abstraction, while novelization is a process of individualization. I hope that, as people, we avoid making up abstractions—stereotypes—about people, places, or things (all southerners are slow, all northeasterners are rude, or all Californians are so laid-back they might as well be nerve-gassed) or at least we realize what a dangerously reductionistic practice that is. Yet the critic's (and particularly the theorist's) living is earned by doing just that with the texts he or she finds (asserting that all nineteenth-century novels end in death or marriage, all art is moral, or all epics begin *in medias res*). It's important to remember that there is more reality to an individual text than there is to an individual theory about a text.

At the same time we have to realize we cannot do away with theory altogether. Theory is a process of abstraction, and abstraction is a process of categorization, and—to make an extremely *un*postmodern point—we cannot think or communicate or probably even survive very long without categories; because through them, we make sense of our existence. There has to be a little bit of Aristotle in us all to help us get along from day to day. Without categories we would all become in a real way hebephrenics—and, deconstruction notwithstanding, such incoherence would surely pose a basic problem when we need to brush our teeth, collect our paychecks, feed our children, and stop for red lights. We must, therefore, do two things simultaneously: we must realize that we are drawing road maps and that without road maps we are bound to get lost; and we must recognize that road maps *are* road maps and that we can't drive *on* them but *with* them (and that we *still* might get lost). Theory, then, is good, but it doesn't prevent things from happening.

33

Second, writing about something is not the same as embracing that thing. Alas, it is an evident point but one that apparently needs accentuating; for some reason, critics tend to equate other critics with what they study. If one studies existentialism, then, one must be an existentialist. If one studies structuralism, one must be a structuralist. When it comes to the study of postmodernism, the trend is particularly pronounced. Because I am *studying* postmodernism, I must *be* an apologist for postmodernism. In truth, that needn't follow, and in my case it does not. I neither intend my study to be a manifesto for postmodern comedy nor an attack upon it. Rather, I intend it simply to be a description. In my first chapter I lay out my theory for postmodern comedy, and in the following chapters I explore how that theory is manifested (or not manifested) in various texts. Just because I am writing about postmodernism does not mean I am obliged to write postmodernly any more than a critic writing about Chaucer would be obliged to write in Middle English. In fact, I generally discuss postmodernism in an essentially Cartesian rational linear discourse because that is the one likely to reach the widest audience.

Third, as I have already suggested, every narrative strategy can suggest a metaphysical one. So can every critical strategy. If so, then every piece of criticism or theory becomes a piece of autobiography. I hope my autobiography will reveal my sense of fascination before my subject, but I am also well aware that many of the critical strategies I employ—notions of periodization and genre, for instance—are "totalizing" systems that fly in the face of what it is I am trying to describe: postmodern humor, a detotalizing impulse that embraces plurality. Ironically, then, I am using maps to plot out a labyrinthine city whose planners do not believe in maps; that does not mean, however, that maps are useless in finding one's way around the city.

Gravity's Rainbow

I now turn, in the four remaining parts of my book, to seven fiction writers through whose projects I will explore various aspects of the arc—gravity's rainbow—of postmodern humor.

In the first part to follow, "Displaying the Giants," I will develop a norm by which to gauge the texts in my study by looking at a self-proclaimed late modernist, Guy Davenport, and his collection of short stories, *Da Vinci's Bicycle*. Here I will further delineate the distinction between modernity and postmodernity by arguing that modernism can be seen as a renaissance of the archaic and that, by implication, postmodernism can be seen as a failure of that renaissance. I will also discuss the marginalization of the humorous in modern texts.

In the second part, "Sawing the Clown in Half," I will focus on two writers of the late fifties and early sixties whose texts teeter between modern and postmodern consciousness, unsure of which vision to accept. First, I will examine how Vladimir Nabokov deconstructs certain modern assumptions in *Lolita* while trying to embrace others and uses a common postmodern metagenre—the fantastic—to do this. Second, I will look at how Anthony Burgess in *A Clockwork Orange* subverts some of his own moral intentions by unconsciously generating a highly unstable text. Both works attempt to be satiric in nature, but both fail to locate a communal sense of values on which to base their satire.

In the third part, "Mindcircus in Motion," I will examine the culmination of the postmodern humorous impulse in works produced in the sixties and seventies. By examining a seldom discussed text, Samuel Beckett's *How It Is,* I will demonstrate the ways in which postmodernism has turned its sense of joking against itself and against its readers—the final centers of authority in this century. Then, using a number of texts by Donald Barthelme, I will explore how postmodern comedy, in an act of Bakhtinian carnivalization, transforms language itself into a heteroglossic schtick. I then pull back and summarize the personal and cultural assumptions that lie behind such postmodern humorous gestures.

In the fourth part, "Outside the Bigtop," I will discuss the first moves away from postmodern humor in the early 1980s, an increasingly conservative era marked by the Reagan-Thatcher-Kohl axis. First, I will discuss the rise of pragmatism and politics in D. M. Thomas's *White Hotel* and how such concerns serve to interrogate the essence of postmodern humor. Second, I will show how a text such as Walter Abish's *How German Is It* both tries to buy into the basic orthodoxy of postmodernity in terms of its techniques and at the same time unconsciously begins to move away from that orthodoxy in terms of its subjects and themes. Third, I will conclude by suggesting that, as we move into the last decade of our century, both postmodernism and the comic vision have once again been marginalized by our neoconservative culture.

The Raw and the Cooked

Two guiding metaphors will summarize my approach in this study. The first is one used by Claude Lévi-Strauss at the beginning of *The Raw and the Cooked* when he describes the optical microscope. Although the instrument cannot give the viewer the whole picture of matter's structure, he says, it can give the viewer various degrees of enlargement. Each degree "reveals a level of organization which has no more than a relative truth and, while it lasts, excludes the perception of other levels" (3).

The second is the metaphor Kathryn Hume uses to introduce *Pynchon's Mythography,* her study of *Gravity's Rainbow.* She asserts that interpretations of the same text might appear very different from one another but that, in the end, each might be perfectly valid in its own right. Think, she suggests, of a human torso. That torso may be rendered as an impressionist painting, a cubist collage, an X ray, a thermogram, an ultrasound scan, or a CAT scan. Each is a valid way of representing the torso and, to the untrained eye, seems unrelated to the others and perhaps even contradictory. Yet, to Hume, "these realities coexist and more or less complement each other; furthermore, no one of them should be taken to represent an exclusive reality. . . . The more such renditions we can draw on, the richer will be our grasp of the realities they represent" (32–33).

My own approach will be multiperspectival in nature. I will render each text or textual complex in a way (or ways) I feel interestingly illuminates it for the reader. And rendering a text interesting—maybe even fresh and alive—for the reader strikes me as the ultimate goal of most criticism, or, at least, most of the criticism that I enjoy. Now, these ways of illumination need not be in divine harmony. I understand that much ink has been spilt proving that structuralists shouldn't be bed partners with biographers, who most definitely shouldn't be bed partners with New Critics, who most definitely shouldn't be bed partners with just about anyone. Such rigid compartmentalization, however, seems to me antithetical to the way the world and texts work. It is certainly antithetical to the way the postmodern comic vision works. As Lang points out, the humorous critic "values the criterion of exhaustivity (a reading must take into consideration as many elements of a text as possible) above that of univocity" (8). For better or worse, for me, interpretation need not be so much an exclusive project as an inclusive one, and a joyous project, at that. I suppose I am back again to my loose baggy monster. And it seems as good a time as any to begin scratching him under his furry chin to make him purr.

II
DISPLAYING THE
GIANTS

2.

A Guydebook to the Last Modernist, or: The Renaissance of the Archaic

> The rule was: everything in its place.
> —Davenport, *Geography*

Modernism and the Conservatives

I first met Guy Davenport in March 1985 during my on-campus interview for a position in the English department at the University of Kentucky. What struck me initially was that the polymath was wearing a trim three-piece suit the color of burnt umber and socks the color of lobsters and that the socks kept peeking out from beneath the polymath's slacks as he sat on the couch across from me, imposing, arms folded across his chest. Then followed his brown eyes, penetrating as Kafka's, and his European charm—and his European aloofness. Then followed an offhand comment he made in the middle of a conversation we were having about the difficulties of trying to pin down such an amorphous term as *postmodernism*. We had been speaking for a while about Kenneth Gangemi (whom Davenport admires) and Walter Abish (whom Davenport doesn't) and then Davenport said that, though he could intuit a difference between the *modern* and *postmodern*, he had no idea about what such terms actually meant. After all, he said, some critics considered *him* a postmodernist. And then there was John Barth, who recently had called him the last of the modernists. And then the conversation moved back to underwater plants or the Dogons or some such thing as though nothing very special had happened.

For Davenport modernism is "a renaissance of the archaic" (*Geography* 334). In other words, it is T. E. Hulme's Imagist insistence on "classical" hard, clear, precise poetry. It is Picasso's use of the cave paintings at Altamira. It is Gertrude Stein's cutting "her hair short to look like a Roman emperor and to be modern" (*Da Vinci's Bicycle* 59) and Charles Olson's use of the epsilon on the omphalos stone at Delphi in "The Kingfishers." It is even the echo of Democritus in Niels Bohr and Heraclitus in Ludwig Wittgenstein. In many ways, it is T. S. Eliot's "mythical method," which he defined in his 1923 review of Joyce's *Ulysses* as the "manipula[tion] of a continuous parallel between contemporaneity and antiquity," and which he used the year before in *The Waste Land* to order and give significance to a modern world he saw as an "immense panorama of futility and anarchy" (11–12).

It was a renaissance that began around 1910 and was over by 1916 because World War I had "blighted" a cultural rebirth "as brilliant as any in history" (*Geography* 166). Except for those who were at that time already modernists moving toward full maturity (Joyce, Pound, and Eliot, for instance), the twentieth century ended before its second decade was done. By implication, what has come to be called postmodernism is in a way the failure of the renaissance in our century. And for Davenport *postmodernism* is a particularly apt term since it suggests a between-times, a lack of clear purpose, perhaps even a return to a kind of barbarity: "Olson's *Maximus* and Zukofsky's 'A' are too symbolically and verbally complex, respectively, to command large audiences, especially in an age when a college degree is becoming a certificate of illiteracy" (one hears Eliot's ghost here, loud and clear [*Geography* 317]). Like Yeats, Davenport believes "we do not . . . live in an epoch; we live between epochs" (*Geography* 309). Like Henry James, he believes we have "let the fire die in the engine" (*Da Vinci's Bicycle* 60). He would probably agree, then, with George Steiner, who argues that with postmodernism "the house of classic humanism, the dream of reason which animated Western society, have largely broken down. Ideas of cultural development, of inherent rationality held since ancient Greece and still intensely valid in the utopian historicism of Marx and the stoic authoritarianism of Freud (both of them late outriders of Greco-Roman civilization) can no longer be asserted with much confidence" (ix).

With this in mind, John Barth's claim begins to make some more sense. Davenport (fiction writer, essayist, poet, editor, illustrator, librettist, translator of classical Greek, and scholar, but "primarily a teacher" who argues that "all my writings [are] extensions of the classroom" [*Contemporary Authors*]), is the "last modernist" to the extent that he is one of the last of a generation to have been influenced more profoundly by creators such as Pound, Picasso, and Joyce than by those such as Ashbery, Warhol, and Robbe-Grillet. (Of course, he is not *the* last, Barth's statement notwithstanding; one thinks of writers such as Julian Barnes, Doris Lessing, and William Gass, the last of whom even refers to himself as a "purified modernist.") Davenport is, along with Marx and Freud, one of the late outriders of classical humanism. Along with them he dreams the dream of cultural development and inherent rationality that once animated Western society. His fictions share the modernist belief in a transcendental signified of fragments shored against the ruins, in the omnipotence of language, in the archaic. Like his creation C. Musonius Rufus, those fictions are "damned to sanity and hope" (*Da Vinci's Bicycle* 32).

For Davenport "the universe is harmonic or it wouldn't work. Heraclitus [and here recall the epigraphs to 'Burnt Norton'] announced almost three thousand years ago that the harmony of the universe, that is, of everything, is hidden. The duty of philosophy is to find that harmony" (*Every Force* 108). As Robert A. Morace points out, Davenport follows the modernist notion that life is a work of art, thereby creating a work that is moral in John Gardner's sense of the word. Davenport's work "takes both as its method and as its subject that 'process'—the voyage in search of (or in the creation of) affirmative human values—which characterizes 'moral [and modernist] fiction' " (72). In this way, Davenport's vision is—like modernism's in general (and, for different reasons which I have already discussed, like neorealism's)—primarily a conservative one. It is concerned with conserving a way of thinking, a mode of consciousness, a system of values that may have come to dominance in our culture in the late nineteenth- and early twentieth-century but have always been around in one form or another. In the great humanist tradition, Davenport's vision self-consciously looks backwards rather than ahead for its support and its inspiration. And so Davenport would surely agree with Huyssen's "traditionalists in the academy or the museum for whom there is still nothing new and worthwhile under the sun since the advent of modernism" (199).

That there are *ten* stories in his second collection, *Da Vinci's Bicycle* (1979), is then significant because ten is the perfect number, one which holds the other nine within itself—three for the soul, four for the body, and seven for the complete man. Saint Augustine argues that divine law is indicated by the number ten. Ten is the basis of our numerical system. Though we speak in many languages and write in a tangle of scripts, for all scientific work there is only one system, and it consists of ten symbols, and all other numbers can be expressed by means of these two handfuls of signs. Ten is also the sacred number for the Pythagoreans, a number that was symbolized by the dotted triangle (*tetractys*), the source and root of all nature. Ten is the signal of reason, culture, the possibility of coherence. It is the announcement of the transcendental signified.

The Geography of *Da Vinci's Bicycle*

In his essay "Narrative Form and Tone," Davenport paraphrases Boris M. Ejxenbaum (and Davenport often returns to the Russian formalists in his writing), saying that "short stories tend to accumulate along thematic lines" (*Geography* 316), and the overarching theme of *Da Vinci's Bicycle* is suggested by another observation by Davenport, this time about his youth: "I spent my childhood drawing, building things, writing, reading, playing, dreaming out loud, without the least comment from anybody. I learned later that I was thought not quite bright, for the patterns I discovered for myself were not things with nearby models" (*Geography* 366). As with Davenport the child, all the characters in *Da Vinci's Bicycle*—all the characters from history, many from Western civilization's childhood—spend their time drawing, building things, writing, reading, playing, dreaming out loud, without the least comment from anybody. They are all pioneers somehow out of step with their contemporaries—ignored, bullied, or misunderstood, invariably thought not quite bright, even silly, because the patterns they discover in the world are not the patterns that their contemporaries discover.

The alpha fiction, "The Richard Nixon Freischutz Rag," is about the blurring of fact and fiction and the geography of three imaginations. All are, as the title hints, freeshooters who enjoy jazzy solo performances. And all are explorers, inventors, detectives (detectives of ontology and epistemology, it should be noted, abound in this work) searching out various harmonies. Richard Nixon reverses the path from east to west that Western civilization took and flies to

China in 1972 to meet with Chairman Mao in order to reunify east and west. He is the politician, a figure who will turn up frequently in the following fictions (Nero, Mussolini, Napoleon), usually in the form of megalomaniacs, usually dangerous, here with an astoundingly prosaic imagination. All the scenes having to do with Nixon, as Davenport informed me in a letter written on 10 July 1986, "are real, as reported in a biography of Kissinger. [They] only *sound*[ ] like satiric fiction." When shown the Great Ten Thousand Li Wall, all Nixon can say is: "I think you would have to conclude this is a great wall" (*Da Vinci's Bicycle* 1). When read a poem by the artist Mao, he responds with: "That's got to be a good poem" (2). When speaking with the Chinese leader, he metamorphoses into an absurd gremlin-like tourist who "sank too far into his chair, his elbows as high as his ears" (9).

But below the silly prosaism pulses a destructive imagination as well—one that, before flying to China, orders a hundred and twenty-five squadrons of B-52s to bomb the DMZ in Vietnam because it knows "Chairman Mao would be impressed by such power" (5). Such a twentieth-century mind is juxtaposed to the poetic and creative mind of the fifteenth century when in the second section there appears Leonardo thinking about Paola Toscanelli, an astronomer, physician, and geographer who saw Halley's comet in 1456 and apparently encouraged Columbus to strike out into the Atlantic. Nixon's flat, hard, tough mind gives way to a mind that thinks of the Earth "round as a melon, plump and green" and believes "the world was knit by prophecy, by light":

> Meadow grass from Fiesole, icosahedra, cogs, gears, plaster, maps, lutes, brushes, an adze, magic squares, pigments, a Roman head Brunelleschi and Donatello brought him from their excavations, the skeleton of a bird: how beautifully the Tuscan light gave him his things again every morning, even if the kite had been in his sleep. (3)

Leonardo, who delighted in imagining the machines of war—in 1482 he sent a letter to the regent of Milan with plans for armored tanks, cannon, catapults, and various traps—and who left his most famous work unfinished (*The Last Supper* and *The Mona Lisa*), here works with Salai, his young assistant and beloved (who will become a third-rate painter), on a "two-wheeled balancing machine" (4), the drawing that appears on the title page of the collection and that "is derived, with structural reinterpretation in the fork and seat strut, from Antonio Calegari's model in Augusto Marinoni's 'The Bicycle' " (xi). This is what Hugh Kenner calls the Cartesian Centaur (117–32), a bicycle a man will ride, a machine in harmony with the human, a mechanical body that allows the Cartesian mind to balance atop it. It is also an image that reinforces the idea that in these short stories "everything is on the line between Fact and Fiction" (Davenport's 10 July 1986 letter). Leonardo searches everywhere for a binding force, something that will pull the microcosm and macrocosm into accord. He looks at a blade of grass and sees the universe: "And in the thin green veins ran hairs of water, and down the hairs of water ran light, down into the dark, into the root. Light from the farthest stars flowed through these long leaves" (4–5).

The relationship between Leonardo and his beloved rhymes with the set of homosexual lovers in this short fiction, Gertrude Stein and Alice B. Toklas. Their section, like many in this collection, proceeds by indirection. Stein is never named, and Toklas is referred to only as Alice. In his essay on Max Ernst, Davenport mentions that Victor Shklovsky "felt that art served a purpose by 'making the familiar strange,' a process of regeneration (of attention, of curiosity, of intelligence) the opposite of narcosis" (*Geography* 382). He could as well have been describing this section of *Da Vinci's Bicycle* or Stein's fetish for Cubist painting that tries to make one see without conventions—as Davenport indeed will do in "Au Tombeau de Charles Fourier." That the Stein section is the only one in this first fiction told in the first person is fitting. It suggests itself as a new way of seeing, a subjectivity of perception, a twentieth-century pattern without nearby models.

"C. Musonius Rufus" drops us back even farther in time. When Nero's spies brought him word of a widespread conspiracy to overthrow the emperor in AD 65, he put Seneca, Lucan, Petronius, and others to death. At the same time he exiled Musonius, who was one of the most sincere and consistent of the Stoic philosophers in first-century Rome. The Roman Stoics scorned metaphysics and turned instead to a philosophy of conduct whose essence was self-control. Through the subordination of passion to reason, they felt they could attain human decency, family unity, and social order. Perhaps more than any other Stoic, Musonius took this philosophy of conduct seriously. He taught equality for women. He taught that women should be educated. He spoke against gladiatorial games at the circus and insinuated that, by attending them, the emperor was as bestial as the fighters he witnessed. He spoke—like Pound (and Davenport in a letter to me dated 8 July 1985 writes that "the Musonius story is about Ezra Pound")—against taxes (Davenport's *bête noire*), war, slavery of any kind, and even premarital sex. For his trouble he was, as Pound told Davenport (*Geography* 171), first sent to a waterless Aegean island, then to a chain gang.

Elsewhere, Davenport says that "southerners take a certain amount of unhinged reality for granted" (*Geography* 174), and in Musonius's mind there is no doubt that reality has become unhinged, that "the world is mad" (*Da Vinci's Bicycle* 29), and that it is maddest in its politics. Rome "is a shapeless bundle of shitten pissburnt sweatscalded bubonic rotten rags held together with a bronze wire of discipline" (*Da Vinci's Bicycle* 26). Western culture has exiled its philosophers, its creative minds, and has gone rotten in the teeth.

The story of Musonius, who fulfilled his fate while alive, is juxtaposed with the story of Balbinus (AD ?–238), who was assassinated by the Praetorian Guard and who missed his fate. Balbinus tells his story, like Beckett's Unnamable, from beyond the grave. His remains are kept in a jug, and he is literally in search of a self. He is instructed by Daimons (Consiliarii) and discovers death is a spinning, that "to turn is to exist" (11) in this new dimension. The world, in other words, has gone topsy-turvy for him in death just as it did in life. Like Leonardo, he equates light with binding power: "Spirit must be a substance very like light. Old polarity of head and butt no longer maintains" (12). He both leaves and does not leave his jug, having somehow become able to diffuse into the world, to become a part of everything. Even in death. then, he is an explorer. He merges with a tree, hurls into the clouds, chats with donkeys, whirls into the core of the Earth, and darts into a sunflower. And what he finds is that all is off balance, out of proportion: "I see lizards the size of elephants clumping through ferns as big as oaks" (31). And sometimes, hard as he might try to the contrary, the world evaporates and there are "days when I can hear nothing, see nothing, feel nothing. I am loneliest then, and fearful. I have learned to search the white for a yellow dot, which grows if I stare at it, until a gnat-swarm of bilious specks gathers around it and becomes a detail: a horse's eye, a jug of olive oil, a whetstone" (25), and, through an act of imagination, he can pull the universe into being again—a good Cartesian.

Suddenly, this second fiction zigzags into the twentieth century with the intrusion of Mussolini (33), the modern-day Nero. For the Stoics things do not happen in time. Time for them is a dimension of things, and the eternal course of the universe is cyclical, not progressive or regressive. The decay at the heart of the world in the first century is an analogue for the decay at the heart of the world in the twentieth. Things have not progressed or regressed, the structure of the fiction argues. They have spun in a circle. For to turn is to exist.

"The Wooden Dove of Archytas" spins us back several more centuries to Archytas the Pythagorean, dictator of Taras. Archytas believed in a communist aristocracy. He was the man at whom Plato became angry because Archytas was carrying on experiments in mechanics that corrupted the pure realm of geometry. Archytas developed the mathematics of music, wrote various tracts on philosophy, doubled the cube, scribed the first treatise on mechanics. He invented the pulley, the screw, and the baby rattle. As a Pythagorean, he believed that philosophy was a mode of conduct that would lead to the salvation of the soul. At the center of that philosophy was the belief that to achieve salvation man must be in harmony with other forms of life and with the cosmos. That is, Archytas's imagination and that of Aristopolites, the boy who narrates this fiction, rhyme with those of Leonardo, Stein, and Musonius. In an essay called "Finding," Davenport writes that "childhood is spent without introspection, in unreflective innocence. Adolescence turns its back on childhood in contempt and sometimes shame. We find out childhood later, and what we find in it is full of astounding surprises" (*Geography* 361). Such a romantic myth informs "The Wooden Dove of Archytas," a fiction about childlike imaginations that find the world "full of astounding surprises." Archytas invents a wooden dove—some strange echo, perhaps, of Yeats's bird in Byzantium, a wonderwork of art and order—that runs by steam. He puts it together, sets it up, and, in a moment both scientific and mystical, "it whistled up like an arrow from a bow, fluttered with the stagger of a bat, and banking into a long high wheel, soared over the chronometer tower, the fane of Asklepios, the armory, the hills" (*Da Vinci's Bicycle* 45).

This narrative is intersected by another, one set in the backwoods of the South in the nineteenth century, a Faulknerian tale in which an Indian visits some blacks and asks for a matchbox to use as a coffin for her ringdove that died when it ran into a door. After receiving the box, she journeys back with the others for the burial, where the dove's soul ascends. As Robert A. Morace notes, "instead of polarizing primitive myth and scientific discovery, Davenport makes clear, as Whitman and Pound did, that they derive from the same wellspring: man's searching and redemptive imagination" (74). Both subnarratives are tales about the force of the imagination, both are about magic and ascension. And there is at least a hint that there is some Pythagorean transmigration of souls ("The idea that time cannot be reversed is mere Enlightenment dogma, liberal twaddle," says Borgesian Davenport in *Geography of the Imagination* [358]). But here it is a whimsically backwards one, from a once-living dove to a mechanical one. As with Leonardo's bicycle, the living and the artificial fuse to form a new harmony between the animate and inanimate. Another binding in the cosmos takes place.

According to Davenport, "John Charles Tapner" is based on Victor Hugo's account in his diary, and it is the first fiction in the collection that does not wheel through time. The reader moves from ancient Greece and the southern United States in the last story to an island off the coast of France in the 1850s in this one. At the fiction's center is another exile, Hugo, who has fled from Louis Napoleon, going first from Belgium to Jersey and then from Jersey to Guernsey, because he has failed to acknowledge that Napoleon the Third is the emperor of France. He travels to Guernsey to visit the grave of John Charles Tapner, an unknown man on whose behalf he wrote a letter to the Queen of England asking that Tapner not be hanged for allegedly cutting the throat of his mistress, Miss Saujon. Hugo argued against capital punishment "on the lines . . . that two wrongs don't make a right. Says it makes a murderer of society" (51). His visit to where Tapner was hanged and buried on 10 February 1854 makes him into a kind of detective, a searcher, like the reader himself, who is not informed of Hugo's name until the story is half over (52).

Davenport says he learned early in life that "the search was the thing" (*Geography* 366), not the finding, and at the core of this mystery are several murders that are never solved. Though the reader is never sure beyond a reasonable doubt that Tapner committed the crime he was accused of, the people of Guernsey, who resemble Richard Nixon in the first fiction because, like him, they possess prosaic and destructive imaginations, are quick in their conclusions: Tapner and Miss Saujon "were seeing each other in a sinful way. Moral degeneracy in one respect leads to any other" (*Da Vinci's Bicycle* 57). Why society would murder a murderer is also a mystery here. Hugo's exploration of this mystery makes him, like Tapner before him, an outcast. At one point the narrator's wife, Polly, comments, "Your Frenchman, I've been told, has a wife for show and another for the sin of it. . . . What's more, they're all Papists, and not a moral among them" (50). The narrator, Martin, the Queen's provost, does not argue with her. In the imaginations of the prosaic, the idealist is an aberration.

Davenport often generates textual density by creating gaps—mysteries—on the page that the reader must fill. Such a strategy is thoroughly modernist. As Wolfgang Iser explains in *The Implied Reader,* modern texts frequently exploit the use of gaps to attain their desired effect: "They are often so fragmentary that one's attention is almost exclusively occupied with the search for connections between fragments; the object of this is not to complicate the 'spectrum' of connections, so much as to make us aware of the nature of our own capacity for providing links" (280). In addition to these gaps, Davenport writes in his essay on his first story collection, *Tatlin!* (1974), there are three other ways to create textual density: "through a knitting of sound patterns"; "through a knitting of imagery"; and "by evoking names of people and things" (*Geography* 382).

Davenport employs all of these in "Au Tombeau de Charles Fourier." The result is by far the most difficult fiction in *Da Vinci's Bicycle*. Davenport could have been talking about himself when he called Louis Zukofsky "not so much a poet's poet as a poet's poet's poet" (107). "Au Tombeau" is also the kind of fiction that has prompted Jack Sullivan to argue that Davenport's "dizzying collages" are "often impressive in their cleverness and intricacy, but sometimes wearying in their self-conscious erudition" (46), and Robert A. Morace to point out that "Davenport's kind of intellectual play will never appeal to a wide audience" (87). More than a fiction "Au Tombeau" is what Davenport calls an *assemblage* (380), a blend of history, voices, languages, drawings, times, places, and chronologies, all of which serve to produce an "architectonic form" that "absorbs and displaces narrative" (316) so that "the meaning shapes into a web, or globe, rather than along a line" (318). The outcome moves narrative from a horizontal plane of traditional plot to the vertical plane of the lyric, thereby deconstructing the nineteenth-century or, to use Iser's word, "traditional" version of storytelling in which the process of filling gaps is "more or less unconscious" (Iser 280). The realist work transforms into the Cubist, where the whole becomes "a hieroglyph, a coherent symbol, an ideogram" (*Geography* 312). The impetus to construct such a narrative goes back, again, to Davenport's childhood in South Carolina:

> There were summer drives for finding hog plums, wild peaches, and blackberries on the most abandoned of back dirt roads, autumn drives in search of muscadines and scuppernongs, the finding of which, gnarled high in trees like lianas, wanted as sharp an eye as an arrowhead. We were a foraging family, completely unaware of our passion for getting at things hard to find. I collected stamps, buttons, the cards that came with chewing gum, the other detritus, but these were private affairs with nothing of the authority of looking for Indian arrowheads. (361)

Hugh Kenner once called Davenport's projects "self-portraits," (382) and, in a special way, they are. "Au Tombeau," for instance, is a translation into the adult world of the childhood need to forage.

This fiction is composed of thirty sections, each of which is composed of nine "paragraphs," and these, in turn, are composed of four lines—except for the final section, which consists of only two "paragraphs," the last of which is only three lines long. The meaning of each section is not located, however, at the level of "paragraph." In fact, the subject tends to shift in mid-"paragraph," often in mid-"sentence," as though the artist through his art were mechanically and beautifully boxing perfect chunks of chaos until his machine broke down. The reader is left to forage through detritus for the symmetries like the Dogon at the fiction's center, a primitive people of West Africa, who are trying to find God's complete plan of the universe and who "must search forever, never finding" (*Da Vinci's Bicycle* 96). And like Linnaeus, Picasso, Leonardo and the others in this assemblage who "all search[ ] out the harmonies, the affinities, the kinship of the orders of nature" (68), some self-created mythology that unifies microforces into a macroforce. As Davenport tells us, "Au Tombeau" "proceeds like an Ernst collage" and focuses for the most part on seven kinds of foragers, while the sixteen drawings that are interspersed throughout the story "are meant to be integral with the prose of this story (one hears a lot of the *logos* with one's eyes)" and to "turn the text into a *graph* ('to write' and 'to draw' being the same Greek verb)" (*Geography* 379–80).

The first foragers here are Gertrude Stein and the Cubists, who search for "a primitive and intelligent way of looking," a "tilting of vision," a "ceasing to pretend that we see with our heads in a clamp" (*Da Vinci's Bicycle* 67). Next are the wasps who are "out to forage," "memorizing with complex eye and simple brain the map of colors and fragrances" (64). Third come the Dogon and their god of foraging, Ogo, who, like the Pythagoreans—and like all the other foragers here and elsewhere in this collection—seek to understand "the system and the harmonies" (65). Fourth comes Charles Fourier, a utopian socialist who believed that, because men had been created by a benevolent god and yet allowed themselves to wallow in their misery, they had failed to carry out the divine plan, according to which happiness would replace misery, unity would replace division, and harmony would replace civilization. To accomplish this, Fourier argued, humanity would have to be reorganized into phalanxes (like wasps) of eighteen hundred men, women, and children. Here every person would find a use for his or her special talent, and all would live and work communally and contentedly. Fourier's life became an extended search to develop a single trial phalanx, and along the way he denounced the exploitation and the lies inherent in family, church, society, and state—and in commerce most of all. The next foragers are the flying machines of Bleriot and the Wrights, who again attempt like Archytas and Leonardo to join the animate and inanimate into some larger whole. Sixth is the photographer (and the idea of photography will be picked up in the eighth story of this collection) Lartigue, who quests after a way to see the world differently, to make us see the universe in a new light, a man trying, like Wittgenstein, "to get us to wake up in the midst of dreaming" (*Geography* 311). Last is Davenport himself, both as a character in the assemblage who recounts his visits with Samuel Beckett and his trip to Fourier's tomb, and as the overarching imagination outside the assemblage conceiving all the other imaginations; he is the ultimate forager, that "single intelligence" William James discusses that "permeates [the assemblage's as well as the world's] every part, from the waves of the ocean to the still hardness of coal and diamond deep down in the inmost dark" (*Da Vinci's Bicycle* 60).

"The Haile Selassie Funeral Train," a fiction, like the last four, in which death pulses at the heart, proves what Davenport will have Robert Walser say in the collection's final story: "everything is an incongruity if you study it well" (163). Though it soon turns into a web of contradictions that catches and destroys the facile logic of the wary reader, it appears to begin easily enough. A nameless narrator situated in the present recounts to art critic James Johnson Sweeney a journey that took place in 1936—the trek of Ras Taffari's funeral train on which a number of important figures (including James Joyce and Guillaume Apollinaire) travel but never meet. To this extent, it is a story about what does not happen. But, almost immediately, it transforms into a story about what cannot happen when certain inconsistencies start cropping up.

In *Geography of the Imagination* (which, interesting to note, is dedicated to Hugh Kenner) Davenport admires Kenner, Beckett, and Pound because they are writers who "condense, pare down, and proceed by daring synapses" (382), and "Funeral Train" is a short tight work filled with deliberate gaps. For instance, Ras Taffari, who at his coronation as the Lion of Judah took the name of Haile Selassie, which translates as The Power of Eternity, died in 1975, not 1936. He was the last emperor of a three-thousand-year-old monarchy in Ethiopia, the end of a culture, and hence a fitting image for Davenport to choose, but one which neither Joyce nor Apollinaire knew. Davenport told me that the narrator was no one, just a disembodied voice, but there is also at least a suggestion (the narrator recalls Richmond, Virginia, with nostalgia; he remembers the Blue Ridge Mountains) that another transmigration has taken place, here of Poe's spirit forward in time, or perhaps Davenport's backwards.

By the end of the story, when the reader realizes that the train's trip has been a big impossible circle from Deauville in Normandy through Barcelona, Yugoslavia, Genoa, Madrid, Odessa, and Atlanta back to Deauville, the reader comes to realize he has been on some celestial railroad in a Stoic universe where the power of eternity is cyclical. By implication, the reader finds himself at the end of Western civilization's monarchy and at the beginning of some new Yeatsian second dispensation, but in this between-times, as Apollinaire announces, "we have no shepherds" (*Da Vinci's Bicycle* 113). And the barbarians are on the way: "What in the name of God could humanity be if man is an example of it?" (112). Through a certain optic, this is another fiction about foraging, about the creative imagination (the narrator's, Davenport's) slicing across space and time and reunifying in a startling, metalogical way.

Compared to most of the pieces in this collection, "Ithaka" is a particularly accessible fiction. In many ways it borders on being an anecdotal essay that simply recounts, in the first person, a visit Davenport paid to Pound in Italy (cf. *Geography* 169–76). Narrator Davenport arrives in time to help Ezra move into Olga Rudge's—Pound's companion's—house in an olive grove above Rapallo where she had lived before the Second World War. Afterward, they all go swimming, Pound plunging too far out. They go to lunch, where Pound makes a game of staying wordless, all the while filled with "stubbornness," "glaring and silent" (*Da Vinci's Bicycle* 115).

In earlier days, at St. Elizabeth's Hospital for the Criminally Insane in Washington, D.C., Pound used to talk, but now he can go through a whole day with only a word or two. The title of this fiction suggests the legendary home of Odysseus, the island in the Ionian Sea, where the hero returned after his quests and battles. But this modern Odysseus, this "immensely old man . . . old as Titian . . . standing in gondolas in Venice like some ineffably old Chinese court poet in exile" (115–16), has been hurt by the prosaic world into pain and silence, while his Penelope looks on, hopeful and helpless. The use of the archaic here both connects Pound to what was once most familiar to us as a culture, while reminding us of what we have lost. As Davenport writes in "The Symbol of the Archaic": "behind all this passion for the archaic . . . is a longing . . . for energies, values, and

51

certainties unwisely abandoned by the industrial age" (*Geography* 24)—a conservative nostalgia.

"The Invention of Photography in Toledo" is also less fiction than some strange ratiocinative Borgesian essay. The piece is full of esoterica about the 1826 discovery of photography by Joseph Nicéphore Niepce, the discovery of Uranus by Friedrich Wilhelm Herschel, and descriptions of actual photographs (Lenin in a Zurich café with James and Nora Joyce in the background; those of van Gogh as an adult that only captured the back of his head; the Soviet ones where Trotsky's image has been erased) and imagined ones ("A photograph of Socrates and his circle would simply look like an ugly old man with bushy eyebrows and the lips of a frog" [*Da Vinci's Bicycle* 125]). Yet what it focuses on is a historian of photography—Foco Betún y Espliego (= Focus + Bitumen + Silver Nitrate), the chronicler rather than the chronicle. In 1912 Foco Betún y Espliego abandoned his history of photography to devote his life to getting a shot of the Loch Ness monster. To do so, he becomes an exile, a man who "suffered awful loneliness in his vigil on the gray shores of Loch Ness. The bagpipes ruined his kidneys, the porridge his stomach" (126). What he has done is abandon prosaic photography, the gravity of the mimetic, which emasculates the imagination (and all its universe implies— names, dates, and scholarship), in favor of poetic photography, the buoyancy of the creative, which liberates the imagination (and what its universe implies—magic, timelessness, and swimming dragons).

This pioneer succeeds in giving the lie to the claim that "real life is all that photography has" (123). On a spring day in 1913 Betún traps the image of a plesiosaurus on film. It "shows a long wet nose and lifted lip, an expressionless reptilian gaze, and a gleaming flipper." He has recorded a moment of revelation through what everyone thought was an "objective" medium. But the poetry of Betún is read only as so much prose by the world. The photo "was published in *La Prensa* upside down and in the London *Times* with a transposed caption identifying it as the Archduke Ferdinand arriving in Sarajevo for a visit of state" (130).

"The Antiquities of Elis" purports to be a travel guide written in the second century AD and, more than most fictions in this collection, is composed in a style that registers, as Davenport comments about *Tatlin!,* a "Flaubertian detachment" (*Geography* 382), a style "controlled by artifice" (375). Elsewhere, Davenport notes that "writing in the twentieth century has for its greatest distinction the discovery of the specific: 'Things,' Proust said, 'are gods' " (377). And this fiction is a first-person list of things in Elis, the area in the western

Peloponnesus founded by Aeolus, where Olympia was, and hence where the Olympic games were held for centuries. It is an area famed for its shrine of Hera that goes back to 1000 BC, a shrine whose ruins (fragments of thirty-six columns and twenty Doric capitals still survive) are among the oldest temple remains in Greece, a symbol of the archaic, an echo of Western culture's beginnings: "there is a mortality even in children which we cannot discern in old temples, which, in surviving generation after generation, have taken on that grace by which their sacredness shall probably survive Greece and Rome. Earthquake and impiety cannot destroy them all" (137). Pythagoras visited Elis, as did Thales and Anaxagoras. It is the home of another Sophist, Hippias, who lived in the fifth century BC and taught math and astronomy and protested against artificiality in city life. And it is the home of Skeptic Pyrrhon—"the philosopher . . . who would admit nothing" (138)—who through his student Timon of Philus taught that certainty is unattainable and that, since all theories are false, one might as well accept the myths and conventions of one's own time and place.

All this is recorded by Pausanias, a sightseer, traveller, and topographer, an explorer who wandered through Greece roughly in AD 160 and described it in his *Periegesis* (translated as *Tour*), the first guidebook, consisting of ten books, just as this collection consists of ten stories. Davenport wrote me that " 'The Antiquities of Elis' (though translated from Pausanias, with onions and dust added) is my way of recording a trip across Greece with a young friend in 1960. It is full of private jokes and allusions, and the elder character is my tomcat Max, personified" (8 July 1985, letter). But it is also about how, even in the second century AD, Pausanias senses the loss of the archaic, the decay of our culture, the disappearance of our heritage, our slide toward ignorance. And so his mission becomes an analogue for Davenport's in his fictions and essays—to record the past, fasten down a civilization, and collect and freeze in art what is left of our heritage.

"A Field of Snow on a Slope of the Rosenberg" is an omega of madness that returns us to the twentieth century between the two world wars, just after the failure of the modern renaissance. Paul Cassierer, director of the Neue Sezession art gallery where Robert Walser worked for a time as a secretary, and Walser himself take a hot-air balloon flight from Bitterfeld to the Baltic one windy February. While on their modern epic journey, the Swiss novelist Walser, who was born on Leonardo's birthday, 15 April, but in 1888, and who died in 1956, having spent the last thirty years of his life crazy, drifts into memories about how he conversed one afternoon with Manet's Olympia who spoke to him from a print; how he saw William James accidently dip his tie into a bowl of soup and keep it there so long it began working as a wick; about his time as a servant at Count Rufzeichen's Schloss Dambrau, where he realized that "freedom is a choice of prisons" (157); about an old man's comical heart attack (Walser himself died that way on Christmas Day, while out for a walk); about a Scot who levitates himself and flies out a window; about his work as a bank clerk ("We do not make chairs, we make money. We do not make shoes, we make money" [169]), a soldier ("Our cities are vanishing from the face of the earth. Big chunks of nothing are taking up the space once occupied by houses and palaces" [169]), as author of his masterpiece, *Jakob von Gunten*, which came out in 1908 ("Mann stole it, and Kafka stole it, and Hesse stole it, and were talked about. I have been invisible all my life" [172]).

At one point Walser tells what he calls "my own parable" about the professor at the Sorbonne who electrocuted himself so badly in class that he shot across the lecture hall. When he opened his eyes again, he saw his feet, one on each windowsill of the room. His torso had gone into orbit. His left arm was in the cloak room. His right arm was on a table. What Walser realizes is that the professor "came to pieces. One used the very words" (160–61). What he imagines is the literal fragmentation of modern man. It is a nightmare vision of the twentieth century where modernity becomes "a dream in which confusion has seeped into reality" (171). Back in the balloon "you could not tell whether you sailed past the clouds or the clouds past you." All is a "flip-flop of reality" (150), an Eliotic immense panorama of futility and anarchy, a relativity. And no sane man can stand relativity for long.

For Walser in his balloon the world has become, as Stein said it would earlier in this collection (67), a Cubist painting. The world has become an assemblage just like *Da Vinci's Bicycle*. And, like Pound in "Ithaka," Walser has been hurt into madness by such a recognition. The center cannot hold. He cannot locate the harmonies anymore. Unreality has become his reality. The idea of culture spins away from him. And there is Robert Walser, a forager, an exile, drifting above it all, one of the last modernists, webbing a world in his mind, writing, playing, dreaming out loud, without the least comment from anybody, crazy by everyone else's standards, and, by everyone else's standards, an imp of chaos. "But let us desist," he concludes, tongue in cheek, "lest quite by accident we be so unlucky as to put these things in order" (185).

Everything in Its Place

Guy Davenport's fiction is often funny, Candace Lang would surely conclude, but it isn't humorous. That is to say, Davenport's fiction projects a modern vision that is essentially ironic rather than a postmodern vision that is essentially humorous.

Like the Dogon, like the Pythagoreans, like Leonardo and Hugo and Stein, Davenport is a modern who forages for truth, convinced that with sufficient effort one may in some perhaps slightly more perfect universe than this come to understand the system and the harmonies. Below the surface of things is the Platonic gold of coherence, order, and symmetry. All we need to do is become able enough readers to find the primary and original intention of the work at hand, and here the universe is one more work (*not* text) to be interpreted. The appearance of the work may be deceptive (for in the fiction there may be Poundian silences that need filling, and in the universe there may be Walserian unreality that at first appears chaotic), but interpret it accurately and a valid content will reveal itself.

To phrase it somewhat differently, Davenport's fiction shares the modern belief in the possibility of a metanarrative. It is a fiction obsessed with the search for an elusive transcendental signified, and in this way it rhymes with the work of Yeats who sought a unifying cosmology, with the work of Stevens who sought the Supreme Fiction, and with the work of the surrealists who sought a deeper and richer reality than the sad and fractured mundane one found all around them. And perhaps it rhymes most closely with the work of Vladimir Tatlin, the Russian Constructivist who stressed both the innovative potentials of art as well as its social purpose. Tatlin was one of the first artists in Western culture (his *Relief* appeared in 1914) to create an assemblage from the untreated junk of the culture and to create it with a sense of social reform in mind. So Davenport creates often bewildering, beautiful constructions that at first appear to be against interpretation. Yet for each there is a key that unlocks its heart, and often that heart has to do with one form or another of political injustice. Davenport plays with language, not to display its arbitrariness, but to bask in its power for teaching, for preaching, and for changing. He writes to organize. He writes to conserve. He writes to shore up his fragments against the ruins.

III
SAWING THE
CLOWN IN HALF

3.
A Janus-Text

Reality is a very subjective affair.
—Nabokov, *Strong Opinions*

A Romp Which Does Not Amuse

Vladimir Nabokov called *Lolita,* whose man-
uscript he almost chucked into an incinerator once in 1950 and again
in 1951, his "special favorite" (*Strong Opinions* 15) and said that, of
all his works, he had "the most affection" for it (Appel, "Interview"
44). It was the only one of his novels written in English that he valued
enough to translate into Russian, and he did so in 1967. But when the
novel first came out in Paris (1955), New York (1958), and London
(1959), it certainly didn't look like many reviewers agreed with him.
Contrary to the impression one has reading more recent Nabokov
criticism, which tends to overemphasize *Lolita*'s being turned down
by four American publishers only to be picked up by Maurice
Girodias's Olympia Press in Paris (known for its publication of Jean
Genet and works of pornography), *Lolita* did float up to the top of
the best-seller list and hover there for a year. And many critics—
including John Hollander, Howard Nemerov, Lionel Trilling, and
Kingsley Amis—gave it strong positive reviews. But it also offended
at least an equal number of critics. Many were less than impressed by
what they read. And many were downright hostile.

In *The Saturday Review,* for example, Granville Hicks said *Lolita*
was "not one of the more memorable novels" (38), and, in his *Nation*
review, Robert Hatch said it was "not a very inventive book—beyond
the initial audacity" (563). E. F. Walbridge wrote in *Library Journal*

that "thousands of library patrons conditioned to near-incest by 'Peyton Place' may take this book in stride. However, better read before buying. Although the writer prides himself on using no obscene words, he succeeds only too well conveying his meaning without them" (2183). Such is glowing praise compared to what Orville Prescott thought in the *New York Times:* "there are two equally serious reasons why [*Lolita*] isn't worth any adult reader's attention. The first is that it is dull, dull, dull in a pretentious, florid and archly fatuous fashion. The second is that it is repulsive." This kind of attack has affinities with the one launched by Riley Hughes in *Catholic World:* "[the] very subject makes it a book to which grave objection must be raised. . . . As a study of unnatural infatuation, of a man and mind obsessed, it might be said to have a certain clinical authority. But the aura of evil, the implications of a decadence universally accepted and shared—this is a romp which does not amuse" (72).

At least part of what all of these negative—and strangely charming—reviews may be responding to is the pulse of the fantastic that beats at the heart of *Lolita* and to fantasy's general tendency on a thematic level to present a culture with the very forces it must repress in order to remain successful and functioning. One of the dark strengths of fantasy is that it presents a culture with what it cannot stand, possibilities of alternative universes, possibilities of taboo—in *Lolita* incest, sadism, masochism, murder, and nympholepsy, to name but a few. That is, as Rosemary Jackson claims, fantasy "traces the unsaid and unseen in our culture" (4). Roger Caillois echoes this in *Au Coeur du Fantastique,* when he writes that "the fantastic is always a break in the acknowledged order, an irruption of the inadmissible within the changeless everyday legality" (quoted by Todorov 26). Fantasy becomes a mode of narrative illegality, which is, as Hélène Cixous notices, "a subtle invitation to transgression" (200, my trans.). The theme of the fantastic, then, is an exploration of the limits of civilization, an exploration that along the way dismembers humanist and religious sanctions concerning what is "proper," "decent," and "acceptable" in order to interrogate them at their foundations.

Postmodern Fantasy (and Science Fiction)

The fantastic came into wider and wider use as a "literary" mode of fiction in the first half of the twentieth century as a way of liberating the imagination from nineteenth-century realist and naturalist assumptions. Roughly from the late 1950s through the middle of the 1970s it became something akin to the dominant mode. "Serious" writers as varied as Jorge Luis Borges, Richard Brautigan, Gabriel García Márquez, Angela Carter, and Italo Calvino appropriated the mode in order to explore the possibility that contemporary experience is something that is continually beyond belief, that unreality is the reality that the second half of the twentieth century understands. As Philip Roth commented back in 1961, contemporary experience "stupefies, it sickens, it infuriates, and finally it is even a kind of embarrassment to one's own meagre imagination" (224). The job of the contemporary artist, it follows, is to find ways of responding to a situation that is, literally, fantastic. Little wonder, then, that fantasy becomes the vehicle for his or her consciousness.

By generating alternate worlds that, as Todorov has it, hesitate between the uncanny (where the laws of Cartesian reason and Newtonian science finally win out) and the marvelous (where the laws of Cartesian reason and Newtonian science are finally abandoned), the fantastic raises fundamental epistemological questions: What do I know? How do I know? To what degree is my knowledge about existence certain? And so on. By pointing to worlds that are not there, that only exist in language, the fantastic raises questions about the arbitrary nature of language itself. Although the fantastic in general may be used for purposes of didacticism or escapism (Shakespeare, Bunyan, Tolkien), the extremely self-conscious postmodern fantastic (Kafka, Cortázar, Coover) fastens onto the questions that lie at the mode's heart and exploits them willy-nilly. The result is, as I have argued before, the literary equivalent of deconstruction. That is, postmodern fantasy becomes a mode of radical skepticism that interrogates all we once took for granted about language and experience. It casts our basic assumptions about what we know—or think we know—under erasure.

While I have recently focused on postmodern fantasy's interrogation of epistemology, Brian McHale has focused on postmodern fantasy's interrogation of ontology. By creating heterotopias, McHale argues, postmodern fantasy produces an "ontological dialogue" (79) that raises questions of existence: Which world is this? What is to be done in it? Which of my selves is to do it? And so on. According to McHale, the same is even more true of a subgenre of the fantastic, science fiction, which "is perhaps *the* ontological genre *par excellence*" (59). Considering the work of Ursula LeGuin, Doris Lessing, and cyberpunks such as William Gibson and Pat Cadigan, it seems equally correct to say science fiction is perhaps *the* epistemological genre *par excellence.* Yet, closer to the point would be the assertion that the postmodern fantastic, which includes science fiction, is obsessed with both epistemological *and* ontological questions.

Postmodern fantasy may or may not be funny. We need only remember that Kafka laughed with delight as he read *The Metamorphosis* to his friends, that *Gravity's Rainbow* has been discussed as a comic epic, that readers frequently rejoice in the madcap scenes from texts such as Guillermo Cabrera Infante's *Three Trapped Tigers,* Ishmael Reed's *Mumbo Jumbo,* and John Barth's *Giles Goat Boy.* By definition, however, postmodern fantasy must always be humorous. By definition, it affirms the discontinuity and inherent otherness of the self, language, and the world. It is impossible in postmodern fantasy to "see through" the signifier to the golden signified because, in a very practical way, signifieds do not exist in such a universe of discourse, or they exist in a way radically different from the way they do in traditional realist texts; certainly no referent in the world external to the text exists for the signified. Hence, in postmodern fantasy "meaning" is unfastened; it floats free. In a story such as "Bloodfall" by T. C. Boyle, in which blood begins raining from the sky one day, one can speak of what happens. One can speak of certain conventions, certain textual relationships. One can even, if ironic enough at heart, speak of the proliferation of meaning*s* in the text, the misfirings of the allegorical impulse. But one can never ultimately speak of the Meaning of the text without committing an act of polymorphous perversity.

Reality as a Joke

Now, returning to Nabokov's novel, I do *not* mean to suggest that *Lolita* is necessarily and primarily a work of pure fantasy. As Kathryn Hume convincingly argues, there probably is no such beast. At the root of Western culture a bias has arisen that tends to separate literature along a mimetic-fantastic axis. Plato banished the fantastic from his Republic. Aristotle decided to judge that good literature was that which best imitated reality. And because of this legacy, in many texts the fantastic has been placed almost out of sight, just at the corners of the reader's vision, as that which happens just as one's head is turned. But it is more helpful to say, as Hume does, that "literature is the product of two impulses. These are *mimesis,* felt as a desire to imitate, to describe events, people, situations, and objects . . . and *fantasy,* the desire to change the givens and alter reality" (20).

Rather than an either-or mode of perception, then, one should approach the notion of mimesis-fantasy through a both-and mode. Todorov hints at this when he asserts that the fantastic exists as a "hesitation" between two other modes of discourse, and so does Rosemary Jackson, who suggests we view the mimetic (Todorov's "uncanny") and the marvelous as two poles on a continuum between which, in varying degrees, appears fantasy. The implication of both Todorov and Jackson is that fantasy can be defined at the structural stratum as a mode of discourse that is combined from two other modes, the mimetic and its opposite. To a certain extent, all literature becomes at least in part fantastic and at least in part mimetic. All literature becomes an act of the imagination that attempts both to represent reality and to alter it.

But so far I have been using the word *reality* freely, as though we could all agree on its meaning. Nothing could be farther from the case. In what way, for instance, can we say that a voodoo doctor in Haiti, a stockbroker in Manhattan, and a literature professor in Kentucky share the same sense of "reality"? As Nabokov warns us in his afterword to *Lolita, reality* is "one of the few words which mean nothing without quotes" (314). For him, the notion of consensus-reality—that which allows us to distinguish sharply between fantasy and mimesis—is a dubious one at best. In a 1962 BBC interview, he argues that "you can get nearer and nearer, so to speak, to reality; but you never get near enough because reality is an infinite succession of steps, levels of perception, false bottoms, and hence unquenchable, unattainable" (*Strong Opinions* 11).

Surely one must be wary about constructing a theory, a system, out of the off-the-cuff remarks of a systems-hater. But one should also keep in mind that to begin to speak of terms like *reality* or *perception,* to begin making judgments about literature, is to begin positing theories and therefore to begin implying the existence of systems. Nor are Nabokov's remarks quite as "off-the-cuff" as they might at first appear. In the foreword to *Strong Opinions,* Nabokov explains that, for interviews, "the interviewer's questions have to be sent to me in writing, answered by me in writing, and reproduced verbatim" (xi). In a number of those interviews Nabokov attacks the notion of consensus-reality and even goes so far as to "regard the objective existence of *all* events as a form of impure imagination" (*Strong Opinions* 154). In other words, he considers the idea of a stable communal reality a shady concept at best that may be approximated but not imitated. He hints that it is an ethnocentric notion (and here one should recall that García Márquez has spoken of *One Hundred Years of Solitude* as a realist novel) that is a kind of fantasy, a "creative fancy" (*Strong Opinions* 154).

If one carries this idea to its logical conclusion, as the Borgesian Nabokov did in a 1969 interview with the London *Sunday Times,* one must admit that one does "not believe that 'history' exists apart from the historian" (*Strong Opinions* 138), that each of us produces his or her own fantasy or construction, which he or she then calls "reality." Hence, objective reality is unknowable. Many postmodern writers and theorists have made just such a point. Basing his notions on those of the Flemish philosopher Geulincx, for example, Beckett argues in works such as *Murphy, The Unnamable,* and *Worstward Ho!* that there is no connection between the mind and the external world and that therefore the only reality one can know is one's perception of it (if in fact it exists apart from one's perception of it). Reiterating an idea put forth by two sociologists, Peter L. Berger and Thomas Luckmann, McHale claims that reality is "a kind of collective fiction, constructed and sustained by the processes of socialization, institutionalization, and everyday social interaction, especially through the medium of language" (37).

To translate these ideas from an ontological to a narratological plane is to move from the question of reality to the question of mimesis. It is to move from the question whether there *is* a reality to whether or not one can *imitate* it in art. Because Nabokov essentially believes that communal reality is unknowable, he is also highly suspicious of the literary form that claims to reflect it—that "so-called 'realism' of old novels, the easy platitudes of Balzac or Somerset Maugham or D. H. Lawrence—to take some especially depressing examples" (*Strong Opinions,* 118).

As I have just said, Nabokov, who paradoxically and inadvertently slips at times into the grid of various systems, is dubious of static closed systems like those of Freud, Chernyshevski, or Lenin. In this way, he separates himself from pure moderns such as Yeats, Eliot, and Joyce, who attempted through complex symbolic structures to tame and imprison what they perceived as chaotic experience. For Nabokov "mimesis" becomes just one more totalitarianism of meaning, a system that claims truth, and he makes certain that we know he rejects all totalitarian systems (except, perhaps once again paradoxically, Art itself). He does this, as J. P. Shute has shown, by repeatedly "and preemptively" asserting "the inaccessibility of his text to any hermeneutics" (641) because hermeneutics imply ideology and because Nabokov, as he told Alfred Appel, has "despised ideological coercion instinctively all [his] life" (Appel, "Interview" 21).

Nabokov's fictions continually seek liberation from the gravity of mimesis—an act that registers a creed that is both aesthetic and political. "Freedom of speech, freedom of thought, freedom of art" (*Strong Opinions* 34–35). Both politically and aesthetically, Nabokov does not "give a damn for the group, the community, the masses, and so forth" (*Strong Opinions* 33). Emphasis then falls on the individual's perception—the solitary, the kinetic, the free. From this angle it becomes easy to understand why Nabokov's first book, which he sold in 1923 for five dollars, was a translation into Russian of Lewis Carroll's *Alice in Wonderland,* and that he has been "always very fond of Carroll. . . . He has a pathetic affinity with H. H." (Appel "Interview" 34–35).

Much has been made of Nabokov's affinities with Joyce and his belief in the omnipotence of language, and with Proust and his obsession with memory. But, as with Carroll's, a number of fantasts' reverberations can be heard in *Lolita:* Edgar Allan Poe, to whom Nabokov alludes frequently (see Phillips 97–101; Dubois 1, 7; and Appel, "The Springboard for Parody" 106–43), and whose House of Usher appears in *Lolita* as Pavor Manor; Kafka, whose *Metamorphosis* Nabokov taught at Cornell while writing *Lolita* and whose dark absurdist humor pervades Nabokov's pages; Borges, whose witty tales of ratiocination and terror have much affinity with those of Nabokov, as Patricia Merivale has demonstrated; Robbe-Grillet, whom Nabokov paired with Borges and then wrote, "How freely and greatfully one breathes in their marvelous labyrinths! I love their lucidity of thought, their purity and poetry, the mirage in the mirror" (*Strong Opinions* 44); H. G. Wells, who is "better than anything Bennett, or Conrad, or, in fact, any of Wells's contemporaries would produce" (*Strong Opinions* 103–4); Jules Supervielle, with whom Nabokov was on friendly terms during his years in Paris; and Beckett, who is "the author of lovely novellas. . . . The trilogy is my favorite" (*Strong Opinions* 172).

These writers all share a need to decompose "so-called realism," what Robbe-Grillet has somewhat misleadingly called the Balzacian mode of fiction, a mode primarily interested in the chronological, the psychological, and the fully rounded character and committed to a belief in stable identity and self, in coherence and mimesis. This is a mode, in a word, firmly grounded in reality. The strategy they have frequently employed in their decomposition has been the fantastic, which, because it acknowledges itself as composed of two modes (the mimetic and its opposite), creates a dialectic that refuses synthesis.

The code that passes from text to reader indicates s/he is neither supposed to apply the conventions s/he has learned of the mimetic nor of its opposite, but a combination of the two: a confusing and sometimes frustrating indication at best. In other words, these fantasts—all of whom I would classify as postmodern—use fantasy as a technique to dislocate, to make discontinuous, to subvert.

Umber and Black Humberland

Two universes of time exist in *Lolita*. First, there is the time of *chronos,* communal time that registers chronology, sequence, a change of state, cause and effect. This is the time of prosaism, details, and inevitable death: Balzacian mimesis, nineteenth-century realism. Opposed to this is the time of *kairos,* or divine time, an intensely autistic time that stands outside chronology and signals a changeless state, a disruption of sequence and cause and effect. This is the time of poetry, love, immortality, and the fantastic—the time of medieval romance, fairy tales, legends, myths, surrealist fictions, and so on (cf. Kermode 47–48).

Humbert Humbert keenly feels the pain of *chronos* and longs through Art to attain the transcendental realm of *kairos* that will allow "a negation of time" (Appel "Interview" 32). In his idealized fantasy of Lolita, he can find a "refuge of art" that "is the only immortality you and I may share, my Lolita" (311). Hence, the fantastic serves to undercut the realistic, to short-circuit it by fashioning a realm that refuses the mimesis of time. But the inverse is true as well. The mimetic short-circuits the completion of the fantastic charge, because, in reality, Humbert never attains Lolita, or rather, all he ever really attains is her body, not her soul. The little of her he has is caught up in the ticktock of *chronos* so that, when he sees her for the last time, he realizes she has "ruined looks," "adult, rope-veined narrow hands," "gooseflesh white arms," "unkempt armpits": "there she was (my Lolita!), hopelessly worn at seventeen" (279). The *only* immortality they can share, their stronghold against the clock, their fantastic *kairos,* is in the pages of an ostensibly mimetic text that records the effects of *chronos* on them—scant consolation because they cannot read about themselves frozen in timelessness for they are both dead before those pages are published.

Just as there are two universes of time in the text that deconstruct each other, so there are two universes of character. The first is Balzacian in nature. This universe is peopled by what E. M. Forster called fully rounded characters, resonant with psychology, brimming with the implication that the self is unified and identity is stable over time. Here we find Humbert Humbert (though his name, a silly pseudonym he has created for himself [5], suggests from the outset, by its double form, a kind of mirror world, a split in self, an unstable identity) in torment, in jail, an aging man filling blank pages during the last days of his life, trying to understand and to justify having treated a young girl as an instrument of his will. He possesses a poetic, if warped, imagination that fantasizes at the expense of the real and so must soon recognize that "what I had madly possessed was not she, but my own creation, another, fanciful Lolita. . . . floating between me and her, having no will, no consciousness—indeed no life of her own" (64). He has forced her into fantasy and thereby zapped her of her identity. By doing so, he has transformed her into "the youngest and frailest of his slaves" (62).

We also find Dolores Haze, whose prosaic name reminds us both of the Spanish for *sorrow* (what she must live in) and the German for *rabbit* (a conventional, and here ironic, symbol for fecundity). She is a bubblegum popping, tennisball whacking, American teen queen whom Humbert turns into a transcendental signified, a sign for ineffable perfection, some incarnation of "perilous magic" (136), "the limpidity of pure young forbidden fairy child beauty" (266), "the great promised" (266), a being who is the embodiment of the Keatsian "fair demon child" (174). Dolores is a supernatural nymph—a word that, as *Webster's Dictionary* will tell, indicates not only the minor nature goddesses from Greek and Roman mythology (and therefore a lovely young woman) but also in anatomy the labia minora, in lepidopterisy any of the nymphalid butterflies, and in entomology the young of an insect without complete metamorphis: a pupa. And as critics have often pointed out, for Humbert, Lolita *is* some rare butterfly he makes a sport of hunting down (cf. Butler). She continually and magically undergoes various metamorphoses. Dolores transfigures into Lolita— Lolita the energetic child into Lolita the burned-out adult. Humbert's love metamorphoses into lust, his lust into guilt, and his guilt into grief. The text itself undergoes a series of metamorphoses from autobiography through case study, biography, confession, tale of the doppelgänger, crazy literary criticism, diary, detective story, romantic novel of idealized love, guidebook, and even comic-tragic novel. The result is a heterotopia that, through its form, stresses the instability and multiplicity of "truth" and "meaning."

Such metamorphoses also serve to destablize the notion of identity, of a unified self, while pointing to a second universe of character in *Lolita*—that which is antimimetic. Often Nabokov has attacked what Robbe-Grillet calls "the old myths of 'depth' " (23) inherent in the mythology of mind formed by Freud, that "Austrian crank with a shabby umbrella" (*Strong Opinions* 116) who advances the "standardized symbols of the psychoanalytic racket" (*Lolita* 287), teaching "the vulgar" that "all mental woes can be cured by a daily application of old Greek myths to their private parts" (Appel, "Interview" 22). Nabokov has attacked a hermeneutics that views self and identity as closed systems—the hermeneutics of the nineteenth-century realistic text. He disintegrates this concept by overtly manipulating his characters in the text, giving us fully rounded characters only to toy with them like some despotic and puckish god.

Now it is true that all authors manipulate their creatures. What is different in Nabokov's case is that he makes a game out of drawing the reader's attention to the process, thereby spawning a self-reflexivity that interrogates the idea of Balzacian characterization. With regard to this issue, he has said that he does not believe in the "old-fashioned, naive, and musty method of human-interest criticism" that removes the characters from the text and "then proceeds to examine these displaced characters as if they were 'real people' " (*Strong Opinions* 263). In a well-known pronouncement, he has said that "my characters are galley slaves" (*Strong Opinions* 95). So the reader turns out to be watching not only Humbert watching Lolita, *his* galley slave, but Nabokov watching Humbert watching Lolita, and, perhaps, if the reader continues this hypothetical trajectory, s/he finds him/herself watching him/herself watch them all.

Nabokov sets up fully rounded characters, then, only to parody their fully roundedness, shaping a magical carnival world, inverting traditional narrative strategy so that we see the wonderful mad Wizard of Oz behind his curtain, recalling what Borges has said in a different context, that "these inversions suggest that if the characters of a fictional work can be readers and spectators, we, its readers or spectators, can be fictitious. . . . [T]he universe is an infinite sacred book that all men write and read and try to understand, and in which they are also written" ("Partial Magic in the *Quixote*," *Labyrinths* 196).

Not only is the concept *character* refracted and lost among funhouse mirrors, but so also are the very characters themselves distorted by those mirrors and cast back to the reader darkly and funnily disfigured. In the nineteenth chapter of the second book of *The Red and the Black,* Stendhal steps forward to make his famous claim about the realistic novel. "Well, sir," he says, "a novel is a mirror being carried down the highway. Sometimes it reflects the azure heavens to your view; sometimes, the slime in the puddles along the road" (359). The assumptions here are clear. Words mirror the world, a perfect pristine mimesis is possible, and nothing *but* the world is mirrored in the novel. It is true that in *Lolita* all the particulars of America are reflected, from the slang to the quaint roadside motels. But the reflection isn't quite in line with the dominant culture's construction. Rather, the text warps the image. Dairy Queen becomes "Frigid Queen," and Disneyland becomes "umber and black Humberland" (*Lolita* 168). In other words, Humbert projects his fears and his guilt onto his environment, and so his tour book of America becomes "crippled" (156), and the car he uses "limp[s]" (259).

Humbert's fantasies generate a grotesque landscape peopled by the bizarre and abnormal. Gaston Godin, for instance, is a "flabby, dough-faced, melancholy bachelor tapering upward to a pair of narrow, not quite level shoulders and a conical pear-shaped head which has sleek black hair on one side and only a few plastered wisps on the other" (183). At one hotel Humbert finds "a hunchback sweeping the floor" (225) and at another "three horrible Boschian cripples" playing tennis (237), while a hotel attendant named Frank at one point casually takes off a glove that he always wears on his left hand and reveals "an entire lack of fourth and fifth fingers" and "a naked girl, with cinnabar nipples and an indigo delta, charmingly tattooed on the back of his crippled hand" (247). Even Dick Schiller, Lolita's husband, who has a one-armed sidekick named Bill, was the "veteran of a remote war, was hard of hearing." While speaking with him, Humbert notices "that one of the few thumbs remaining to Bill was bleeding" (275). This carnival-like gallery of the maimed, the incongruous, and the unnatural delineates the America of a William Faulkner and Flannery O'Connor, the misshapen, unconscious projections of an unhinged mind's fantasies, the unraveling of the Balzacian mode.

The proliferation of warping mirrors in the text becomes another parody of Stendhalian realism. Their surfaces reflect not "external," "objective" "reality" but a wacky Barthian amusement park. Lolita's class list (53–54) at first looks like a mirror of America, a surface packed with the names of the melting pot. On closer inspection, however, it uncovers sorcery. It subtly introduces us to Jack and Mary Beale, whose father will accidently kill Charlotte Haze, and to Rose Carmine, whose name points to Quilty's color. It also gives the reader a supernatural *four* sets of twins, mirrors of each other, who suggest the theme of the double that weaves through the novel. It gives the reader Ted Falter, whose last name is German for *butterfly*—a name that signals both the chase theme and the Wizard of Humberland's presence behind the curtain. It also introduces the reader for the first time to McFate, some larger despotic wizard, Universal Contingency himself, who is responsible for Humbert's problems.

At the Enchanted Hunters Motel, Humbert and Lolita find "there was a double bed, a mirror, a double bed in the mirror, a closet door with a mirror, a bathroom door ditto, a blue-dark window, a reflected bed there, the same in the closet mirror, two chairs, a glass-topped table, two bedtables, a double bed" (121). That is, they can't find external reality anywhere. Even the window only reflects *their* world. There is no way out. Rather, like the textual entities they are, Humbert and Lolita are trapped among reflecting surfaces, trapped at some "dead end (the mirror you break your nose against)" (227). This image of solipsism mocks the confessional mode and the possibilities of egoistic Proustian revelation by presenting the self as an autistic entity caught forever among its own silver surfaces; the self also becomes a dead end, a mirror you break your nose against. To echo Caramello's argument, at the very moment the image of reflecting planes deconstructs the self and the possibility of expression, it contrarily expresses a painful longing for the self and the expression its expression has dismembered.

These dislocations of time, chronology, character, self, identity, psychology, and belief in mimesis add up to a larger dislocation of the premises of the Balzacian mode of fiction, which, as Fredric Jameson writes, "persuades us in a concrete fashion that human actions, human life is somehow a complete, interlocking whole, a single, formed, meaningful substance" (12). *Lolita* ostensibly is the autobiography of a madman, a man who has tried and failed to make coherent a fractured existence, who has suffered "a dreadful breakdown" (35) that sent him to a sanatorium early in life for more than a year and from which he was released only to face "another bout with insanity (if to melancholia and a sense of insufferable oppression that cruel term must be applied)" (36). Humbert's is the lopsided Pynchonesque universe of the paranoid where *everything* makes sense, where everything is connected. The notorious number 342, for instance, follows him through the text—first, the number of the Haze house, then the room at the Enchanted Hunters, then the number of motels he and Lolita visit in one year. Clare Quilty, Humbert's double, might be real and might be just another of Humbert's hallucinations; in any case, he leads Humbert on the famous "cryptogrammatic paper chase"

(252) for which he plants hundreds of clues (?) that all fantastically add up to a crazy system of persecution for "the fascinated sufferer" (247). Quilty is first mentioned in the 1946 edition of *Who's Who in the Limelight* (33), just above an entry for an actress whose first name is Dolores. There, full of voodoo, we find that one of his hobbies is "pets" and that, among others, he has written plays called *The Little Nymph, Fatherly Love, Dark Age,* and *The Lady Who Loved Lightning* (Humbert's English mother was killed when he was three when she was struck by lightning on a picnic). The last of these plays is written "in collaboration with Vivian Darkbloom," whose name is an anagram for Vladimir Nabokov himself.

Such "dazzling coincidences that logicians loathe and poets love" indicate not only Nabokov's playful metafictional presence but also the presence of a malignant universe filled with "obscure indications" (213) where, as Oedipa Maas in a parallel universe discovers in *The Crying of Lot 49,* there exists "a hieroglyphic sense of concealed meaning" (13), a Kafkaesque labyrinth from which the characters cannot escape. This is the Balzacian mode turned on its head, the Balzacian mode made into a joke. Everything makes sense, Nabokov tells us, but the sense it makes is ludicrous, possibly horrible.

The Janus-Text

At the core of *Lolita,* then, we find a struggle for power between at least two competing modes of discourse and the two distinct visions they reflect. On the one hand strives the realistic, whose desire is to imitate the world of *chronos* and to embrace all its premises. On the other hand is the fantastic, whose desire is to subvert the notion of consensus-reality. Each mode struggles to dominate the other, to make the Other into the Self, and the result of such a battle on this field is the creation of massive incongruity, a kind of parody of each mode by the other and a radical destabilization of the text so that in the end it is impossible to know how the reader is supposed to approach the whole.

In other words, we have what Michel Foucault has called a heterotopia, the clash of mutually exclusive worlds. "In such a state," Foucault writes, "things are 'laid,' 'placed,' 'arranged' in sites so very different from one another that it is impossible to find a place of residence for them, to define a *common locus* beneath them all" (xviii). Through its radical incongruity, the heterotopia turns text into joke. But here the joke is raised to an ontological and epistemological level as well. The implication becomes that we cannot know the world in which we live, or that we know only that we live in so many mutually exclusive ones that we live in something akin to schizophrenia.

Nabokov apparently attempts to resolve his heterotopia in a higher unity, to make his joke ultimately serious. He does this by locating a larger center that accomodates multiple universes: the very act of creation itself. He tries, in other words, to embrace the vision of late modernism that inherits its premises from writers such as Joyce, Yeats, and Mann, who ultimately believe in the omnipotence of language, the transcendental signified of Art; in the world according to Nabokov, "there can be no question that what makes a work of fiction safe from larvae and rust is not its social importance but its art, only its art" (*Strong Opinions* 33). Ironically, though, at the very moment he asserts the transcendental force of art, the systems-hater deconstructs the power of art to shape a coherent monologic reality. His use of extreme self-reflexivity, his conflation of incompatible narrative modes, and his deliberate generation of uncertainty at narratological, epistemological, and ontological strata all contribute to this deconstruction.

Consequently, we have a text that is not quite modern, not quite postmodern—and yet both at once. We cannot, in other words, view it through an either-or optic. More helpful would be to picture a continuum with pure modernity at one pole and pure postmodernity at the other. If we attempt to locate *Lolita* on this continuum, we find that we have discovered an in-between text, one that stutters between these two modes of consciousness. It is a text that looks both ways at once. McHale refers to such a work as "limit-modernist" (13), but his term implies a chronology of consciousness, and, worse, narrative evolution. Rather, we are dealing with a Janus-text, a kind that can appear at various times and in various places. Beckett's *Murphy* comes to mind, as does Robbe-Grillet's *The Erasers,* Barnes's *Flaubert's Parrot,* and, of course, Burgess's *A Clockwork Orange,* on which I should now like to focus.

4.
Garden of Forking Paths

"What's it going to be then, eh?"
—Burgess, *A Clockwork Orange*

The Paranoia and Anti-Paranoia of Reading

If it is the case that for the postmodern the world is a text, then it follows that postmodernism is a way of reading. Along these lines, Brian McHale distinguishes between the mental processes we have been taught as modern readers, and the attack upon those processes that are undertaken by postmodern texts. Modern reading (Lang would call it ironic reading) demands that the reader discover patterns that underlie the text at hand and lend the text its intelligibility. Hence, in *The Waste Land* we search, following Eliot's clues planted in his footnotes, for the poet's use of Jessie L. Weston's and James Frazer's books on myth, or we discover how, through a certain optic, Tiresias is the "he" who does the police in different voices and thereby unifies the poem. Postmodern or humorous reading, on the other hand, produces a parody of meaning. The "patterns" that postmodern reading generates are "always subject to contradiction or cancellation. The ultimate effect is radically to destabilize novelistic ontology" (McHale, "Modernist Reading," 106).

To cast this in a postmodern's terms, we may think again of *Gravity's Rainbow*. There Pynchon makes his well-known distinction between paranoia and anti-paranoia. Paranoia is the humanist and modern need to make things connect, to discover form, to shape chaos into

73

cosmos. For Pynchon "there is something comforting—religious, if you want—about paranoia," but there is also something dangerous. Paranoia is the creation of systems, and for Pynchon systems—be they multinational corporations or behaviorist laboratories or meaning-making modes of consciousness—spell the end of change and finally cultural, psychological, and physical death on a cosmic scale. Anti-paranoia, on the other hand, is the posthumanist and postmodern delight in the endless production of signifiers without signifieds. It is a state of mind "where nothing is connected to anything" (434). It is the joy in discovering and then exploring and then taking enjoyment in the fact that we live in the equivalent of Pynchon's Zone.

Postmodern reading, then, is a kind of clownish joke played on the reader raised on modern literary assumptions. We can, if we wish, read *Lolita* as a moral and realist novel about a middle-aged pervert who learns to regret the horror he has perpetrated on a (barely) teenage girl. But if we do so we shall miss the presence of McFate, and Nabokov above Him, fashioning a funhouse of puns and numero-logical conundrums and pseudo-Freudian mismappings and various other subversions of mimetic and modern beliefs that are in the end designed to play a prank on paranoid pattern-seekers. *Lolita* simulta-neously gives us harmonics and cacophonously mocks harmonics. Richard Pearce makes something close to the same point when he writes that "Nabokov's diabolical strategy is to create a recognizable world and then undermine or deconstruct every possible vantage from which we might form judgments. In the end he leaves us with a rich and tantalizing verbal surface suspended, as it were, over a black hole" (*Comic Relief* 31). To read the "black-hole" humor of *Lolita* in a modern way is to miss its point, or lack of one.

Dante as Cricket, or: The Intentional Trap

When we turn to a text like Anthony Burgess's *A Clockwork Orange* (1962), which was based on a trip Burgess took to Leningrad and was the author's response to a parliament that claimed that Brit-ish youth should be conditioned to respect the State, we run into exactly the same kind of problem: Do we read this book in a modern way as a moral dystopic satire, or do we read it in a postmodern way as a parody of all centers, including morality? Interpretive strategies in this case are more complicated than usual. For example, Burgess, who has, interestingly enough, given high praise to *Lolita* (Aggeler 40), wrote in *Re Joyce* that "the fundamental purpose of any work of art is to impose order on the chaos of life as it comes to us" (110), and in an interview he said that "choice is all that matters, and to impose the good is evil, to *act* evil is better than to have good imposed" (Churchill 10). If we track this line to its terminus, we already have a modern reading of *Clockwork* laid out for us. Kennard does so and concludes that "Burgess takes us towards the mystery of infinity not the nothingness of the void. He answers the Post-existential premise that the world is irrational by a leap of faith that what we see is mystery not muddle. Each novel . . . suggest[s] a patterned, and therefore meaningful universe" (154).

Such a reading, however, snags itself in the trap of intentionality. As Frye argues, "the Dante who writes a commentary on the first canto of the *Paradiso* is merely one more of Dante's critics. What he says has a peculiar interest, but not a peculiar authority" (5). In other words, the writer might have a notion of what he or she wants to do in a text, but that text either might not do what the writer intended or might do more than the writer intended. In any case, the writer's statement of intention is limited. Burgess might have intended to make chaos into cosmos and show that choice is all that matters, but that is not the same as claiming that that is in fact what his text accomplishes.

Interpretation is further complicated since we are, in a very physical way, not dealing with a stable text when we speak about *A Clockwork Orange*. We have at least four versions of Burgess's book. First is the British version, with twenty-one chapters, published in 1962. Next is the American edition, with the twenty-first chapter lopped off by an editor at Norton, published in 1963, a deal agreed to by Burgess because he "wanted . . . to be published in America, and . . . wanted some money out of it" (Aggeler 35). The third, also the most widely known, is the 1971 film version by Stanley Kubrick ("Lubric or Pubic or some such like naz" [7], Burgess has Alex call him in a 1987 "interview" with his character). Kubrick didn't use the last chapter of the British version and apparently wasn't even aware of it until his film was well into production. To confuse things yet further, in March 1987 Burgess, who "hate[s] having two versions of the same book" (34), allowed *Rolling Stone* to publish the twenty-first chapter separately, thereby making it available to American readers for the first time—though not as part of the actual text. And in May 1987 W. W. Norton published a new American edition of *A Clockwork Orange* that includes the twenty-first chapter. So now the reader must not only decide whether to read *A Clockwork Orange* in a modern or postmodern way but must also decide *which* text(s) to read.

Of course the same could be said about any text with variants, though perhaps the movie version of *A Clockwork Orange* done by someone other than the author presents some peculiar and interesting problems here. But that is just my point. A paranoid modern reader will read the situation as ironic; s/he will attempt to read through the variants in an attempt to find the Platonically stable text. The anti-paranoid postmodern reader will read the situation as humorous; s/he will delight in playing the gaps for all they are worth, in disorienting the Law of Stable Textuality. Neither approach is in any essential way correct or incorrect. Rather, each simply represents a different mode of consciousness at work. Nor is each necessarily mutually exclusive of the other. If we again employ the image of the modern-postmodern continuum, we see how a reader could read a text or part of a text more or less modernly or postmodernly depending on variables such as the reader's cultural orientation, personal history, and biochemical state.

What's It Going To Be Then, Eh?

No matter which text the reader decides to pursue in the case of *A Clockwork Orange,* textual destabilization begins on the first page of the first chapter, where the reader learns that those in charge of the Korova Milkbar

> had no license for selling liquor, but there was no law yet against prodding some of the new veshches which they used to put into the old moloko, so you could peet it with vellocet or synthemesc or drencrom or one or two other veshches which would give you a nice quiet hor-rorshow fifteen minutes admiring Bog And All His Holy Angels And Saints in your left shoe with lights bursting all over your mozg. (1)

In a modern text such as Faulkner's *The Sound and the Fury,* the reader discovers in the Benjy section a limited amount of language that likely strikes him or her as strange at first; on further reading, however, the reader comes to understand s/he is witness to a language that is mimetic of a retarded mind. That is, the reader confronts an essentially hyperrealist text. The only difference between Faulkner's work and a traditionally realist text is that, in Faulkner's case, reality is seen as an X ray whereas, in a Flaubert novel, reality is seen as a photograph. In a modern text such as Joyce's *Ulysses,* the reader discovers artificial language that is nonetheless both easily interpretable in a psychological framework (again, we are simply seeing language at work on the inside of the head rather than the outside) and clearly aware not of its own impotence but of its own omnipotence. That is, it is a confident language that believes in its power to shape and define existence—albeit subjective existence—mimetically.

In *A Clockwork Orange,* on the other hand, the reader discovers a text akin to such postmodern works as Joyce's *Finnegans Wake* or Russell Hoban's *Riddley Walker* in which s/he is given a language unlike any English ever seen or heard before. In a strict sense, the reader confronts a language that is imitative of none that now exists, internally or externally. Rather, s/he confronts the first signs of an *antilanguage* that posits by its very existence both the possibility of alternate realities and the possibility that language may not be the effective tool for shaping and defining reality it once was thought to be.

In Burgess's text the reader confronts "the dialect of the tribe," the dialect of the teenagers and of the nightworld, Nadsat, made of "odd bits of old rhyming slang. . . . A bit of gipsy talk, too. But most of the roots are Slav" (114). For most American readers who know no Russian, this is baffling at best. The reader begins the slightly ungrammatical sentence in full confidence (they "had no license for selling liquor, but there was no law yet against"), but with the word *prodding* the sentence skips a beat. *Prodding* usually means "nudging" or "pushing," but clearly those meanings don't work here. *Veshches* is a completely foreign word. Perhaps one can finagle *milk* from *moloko* and *God* from *Bog,* and, on a good day, *mind* from *mozg,* but that still leaves words like *peet, synthemesc,* and *drencrom,* to wait threateningly on the page. Those who do know Russian can, if quick enough, work out *vellocet* ("drug") and perhaps the wonderfully anglicized *horrorshow,* which in this context clearly can't be *horror show* (rather, it comes from *khorosho,* meaning "good" or "well")—but that is all. Cheaters, of course, can in the American version of the book turn to Stanley Edgar Hyman's "entirely unauthorized" glossary of Nadsat, which he acknowledges is in some part "guesswork" (182). Yet this adds little to the reading process, since to follow this course means one must continually flip backward and forward, disrupting the reading process even further.

True, after a number of pages, or perhaps even a number of readings, the language does begin to reveal itself. And this revelation is the point. Language is continually *revealing* itself, not as a transmitter of meaning, but as *language,* as a translucent surface through which one can only vaguely make out shapes and shadows of sense (again, as opposed to the ironic modern text where one at least theoretically can retrieve a meaning behind each word on the page). It is as though Burgess's concept of language looks back toward Nietzsche's view and forward toward Derrida's that there exists an unbridgeable gap between words and things. Words here are absences of meaning, not presences. Be that as it may, surely Burgess's use of language looks back to Brecht's *Verfremdungseffekt,* whose intent is to make familiar aspects of reality appear strange and, hence, bring about a critical attitude on the part of the audience. And it looks back to Shklovsky's notion of defamiliarization, whose intent is to make strange the world of everyday perception and thereby reawaken the reader's capacity for new vision by disturbing ordinary modes of linguistic discourse.

Burgess's is a language that demands heightened activity on the reader's part. This call for the reader's extra involvement is emphasized both by Alex's repeated use of the phrase "O my brothers" (3, inter alia), which implicates the reader in the reading process, and Burgess's use of the book-within-the-book (21), which draws attention to the fact that the reader is working with a highly artificial and self-reflexive construct. It is impossible to remain passive with this text, impossible to let one's eyes skim over the sentences. To make any sort of sense at all, one must engage the language to an even greater degree than in a modern text. Here that also means one must engage the world of Nadsat. And, after a good deal of time and effort, one will become as conditioned to the language as Alex will become conditioned to nonviolence. That is, the very act of reading transforms the reader into Alex's accomplice.

On the first reading, Burgess's language is as dark, labyrinthine, and seemingly impenetrable by intellect as is the *futureworld* Alex inhabits. We find a claustrophic and decadent universe in which adults control the days and teenagers, or Nadsats (both the Russian for "teen" and, as Anthony De Vitis asserts, an anagram for "Satan'd" [Aggeler 124]), control the nights. It is a topsy-turvy world with "men on the moon and men spinning round the earth like it might be midges round a lamp, and there's not no attention paid to earthly law nor order no more" (14). It is a world charged with sexuality in which the girls, who wear punkish green and orange wigs, sport on their breasts silver badges imprinted with the names of the boys they have slept with before turning fourteen (2–3), and it is a world charged with brutality where Alex and his droogs for fun can attack a "prof type," tear out his false teeth, kick him in the mouth, strip him, beat him, and then comment offhandedly that it was not "too hard of a tolchock really" (5–7), and where, after beating F. Alexander and raping his wife, Alex and his droogs can drive back to town in their Durango 95, "running over odd squealing things on the way" (24). The media have become neutralized and the Earth transfigured into a socialized global village where the droidish middle class spends its evenings watching worldcasts on the television (17) and its days "rabbiting" at, among other places, the Statemarts (36). Illiteracy is the norm and the ungrammatical terseness of posthuman computerese has wormed its way into the unconscious: "Right. Return to door. Me stand on Dim's pletchoes. Open that window and me enter" (59).

Alex is placed into this nightmarish universe. Only at the end of part one, after he has kicked the "prof type," raided a sweets-and-cancers shop, beaten a drunk, had a run-in with Billyboy and his five droogs, stolen a car, invaded F. Alexander's cottage, skipped school, "accidentally" killed the woman with the cats, been chained across the eyes by Dim, and arrested do we learn that Alex is only fifteen years old (74). His name triggers another set of uncertainties. The name is, as Burgess says, "short for Alexander, which means 'defender of men.' *Alex* has other connotations—a lex: a law (unto himself); a lexis: a vocabulary (of his own); a (Greek) lex: without a law" (*1985* 95).

Alex is a name that points to fairly positive attributes. Alex is witty, bright, energetic, and creative. He is a kind of artist. His art is violence, and he fashions it very well. Indeed, he represents the creative impulse gone wrong—perhaps the evil that is necessary in any creative enterprise. In his own mind he connects images of brutality with those of beauty. When he lies in his bed listening to the new violin concerto by the American Geoffrey Plautus, he imagines "such lovely pictures. There were vecks and ptitsas, both young and starry, lying on the ground screaming for mercy, and I was smecking all over my rot and grinding my boot in their litsos" (33). Dreaming of beating and rape, he orgasms.

For the first third of the book Alex is victimizer, and the reader, although tempted to do otherwise, distances himself or herself from Alex. For the second two-thirds of the book, however, he is victim, and slowly the reader begins to sympathize with him. In many ways, this structure appropriately nods in the direction of *Frankenstein*, the first "official" science fiction novel of them all. Alex is a kind of technological monster created by a myopic society in general and the behaviorists performing the Ludovico Technique in particular. He is the product of a science that is out of control. He is alienated from others, is constantly misunderstood, and is treated as a subhuman freak. Slowly, the reader comes to realize in Burgess's, as well as in Mary Shelley's, text that the monster has his own narrative for what has happened. Rejected by his parents as Frankenstein's monster was by his creator, Alex comments: "I know how things are now. Nobody wants or loves me. I've suffered and suffered and suffered and everybody wants me to go on suffering" (137). Like Frankenstein's monster, Alex begins to sense that "death was the only answer to everything" (141). And like Frankenstein's monster, as F. (an initial that also helps call to mind Shelley's crazed doctor) Alexander understands, Alex is "a victim of the modern age" (157). Consequently, as Burgess informs us in *1985,* we are to find Alex "sympathetic, pitiable, and insidiously identifiable with us, as opposed to them" (95).

But this is only half the story, only one possible partial narrative. Although Burgess may have intended us to feel sympathy and pity for Alex, Burgess's text produces a much more complicated emotion on our part. After all, on the heels of Alex telling about how much he has suffered, his parents's surrogate son, Joe, immediately and correctly points out to Alex that "You've made others suffer. . . . It's only right you should suffer proper" (137). And on the heels of F. Alexander's telling Alex that he was a victim of the modern age, the writer goes on in the same sentence quite rightly to point out that his wife, whom Alex raped and beat to death, was also a victim of the modern age (157). That is, this narrative world isn't as neat as the reader—or perhaps even Burgess himself—might like it to be. Alex is *insidiously* identifiable with us. He might be an artist, and he might be a victim, but he is also, for whatever "justifiable" reasons, a thief, a thug, a rapist, and a murderer. As the "professor type" (whose presence doubles that of the "prof type" Alex and his droogs tolchocked in part one) tells Alex at the end of part two: "You made your choice and all this is a consequence of your choice. Whatever now ensues is what you yourself have chosen" (127).

The romantic idealist might argue that through the course of the novel Alex has been made into a "clockwork orange." The term is taken from the cockney phrase "queer as a clockwork orange," meaning "the strangest thing imaginable," although one should also recall that in Malaya, where Burgess spent a number of years, the word for "human being" is, significantly, *orang.* A clockwork orange thus suggests "the application of a mechanistic morality to a living organism oozing with juice and sweetness" (*Rolling Stone* 76). The pragmatist might well counter, however, by pointing out that it is dim Dim who wears Percy Shelley's mask (21), turning himself into an unconscious parody of the romantic idealist, and the pragmatist might well ask what we are *supposed to do* with such a calculatedly cruel and destructive member of society as Alex when he decides to turn his horrific creativity against the foundations of that very society.

Society takes away Alex's physical and psychological freedom because Alex took away, to one degree or another, the physical and psychological freedom of a number of other innocent people. At first, of course, the reader is tempted to side with F. Alexander, who writes that "the attempt to impose upon man, a creature of growth and capable of sweetness, to ooze juicily at the last round the bearded lips of God, to attempt to impose, I say, laws and conditions appropriate to a mechanical creation, against this I raise my swordpen" (21–22). But if the reader doesn't become suspicious of F. Alexander's purple prose, which itself "ooze[s] juicily," he or she should certainly become suspicious of F. Alexander's hypocrisy. He stands up for his idealistic (and sexist) principle that "a man who cannot choose ceases to be a man" (156) right up until the time he begins to use Alex for his own propaganda. He stands up for his idealistic principle right up until he learns that Alex is responsible for his wife's death. Then he tries to kill Alex. It is not with a little relief that the reader finds out from the minister of the interior that F. Alexander "has been made with desire to stick a knife in [Alex]. But [Alex] is safe from him now. We put him away" (177).

The reader is also tempted to side with the prison chaplain, who, almost word for word, echoes F. Alexander's position, saying that "when a man cannot choose he ceases to be a man" and stressing that "goodness comes from within" (83). But the reader learns to be careful here as well. First, the very fact that through the overlay of phrases the prison chaplain is associated with F. Alexander should call into question what the chaplain says. Second, though the reader might think of the chaplain as a religious voice because of his position at the prison, Alex equates the man with a sad clown, repeatedly referring to him as the "charles" chaplain (94, inter alia). Third, for all the high ideals the chaplain expresses about individual freedom, he speaks in the voice of the state when he patronizingly refers to Alex as "little 6655321," an anonymous number (95, inter alia). Finally, the reader should at least seriously question the ideals spoken by a man "smelling loud and clear of a fine manny von of expensive cancers and Scotch" (94), since "cancers" suggest the very middle class that both Burgess and Alex despise and "Scotch" that the "charles" chaplain is a drunk.

It therefore follows that, appearances notwithstanding, the moral center of the text is highly unstable. The reader cannot side with the individual who is both wonderfully creative and a deadly criminal. Nor can the reader side with the state or the science of the state, which is both rightly protecting other individuals from a person out of control and wrongly denying that individual his freedom by doing so. Such a general sense of uncertainty is reflected at a number of textual levels, from the ambiguous doppelgänger relationship between F. Alexander and Alex to the confused pattern of black and white imagery that appears throughout the novel (the doctors are whitejacketed and the police station is whitewashed, for instance, but so is Alex's favorite drink, moloko, and the statue of Beethoven that he steals; the prison chaplain is dressed in black, but black is also the color of night, Alex's special time).

Burgess may believe that "duality is the ultimate reality" (Aggeler 44), but duality implies a clarity of vision, the certainty held in a binary opposition. *A Clockwork Orange,* on the other hand, comes closer to believing what Dr. Brodsky believes: "Delimitation is always difficult. The world is one, life is one. The sweetest and most heavenly of activities partake in some measure of violence—the act of love, for instance; music, for instance" (115). The world is less composed of two radically separate elements than of some infinitely complex and uncertain conglomeration of indistinct elements. Obviously, as always, the reader must take what Dr. Brodsky has to say with a grain of salt, however, since he is associated with the Ludovico Technique, the closed inhumane system that suggests death itself.

In the traditional text it is not uncommon for such uncertainty to occur throughout the course of the narrative, but the uncertainty usually takes a binary form (the evil Robert Lovelace and the good William Morden in *Clarissa,* the bourgeois materialism of Charles Bovary and the romantic idealism of Emma in *Madame Bovary*) and it is usually resolved by the end (good overcomes evil in *Clarissa,* materialism overcomes idealism in *Madame Bovary*). In Burgess's text this is not the case. In fact, perhaps the greatest unintentional uncertainty centers around how *A Clockwork Orange* is supposed to end. Its conclusion is not at all conclusive. If the reader runs with the original American version and finishes with the twentieth chapter, he or she is liable to read from an open, postmodern perspective. That there are six chapters in part three, as opposed to the seven in part one and the seven in part two, seems to suggest the asymmetrical shape of indecisiveness. Alex jumps from the window of his prisonworld, spins into "a long black black gap" (169), and wakes up in a universe of "all bandages and wire cages" (170) that exists in the "all white" hospital, which smells "all like sour and smug and clean" (169); he wakes, in other words, from one prisonworld to discover himself in another. D. B. da Silva, Something Something Rubinstein, and Z. Dolin are waiting by his bedside, and, when Alex regains consciousness, they tell him: "You have killed those horrible boastful villains' chances of re-election. They will go and go for ever and ever. You have served Liberty well." But Alex knows better. "If I had died," he says, "it would have been even better for you" (171). He has not served Liberty well. He has simply been made the tool of one more system. Indeed, there is the strong possibility that, in order "to put him right," they have "been playing around with inside like [Alex's] brain" again (174).

Alex hasn't so much been *de*conditioned as *re*conditioned, made from a "good" into an "evil" clockwork orange. The minister of the interior bribes Alex to help the very system that originally dehumanized him ("We shall see to everything. A good job on a good salary" [178]), brings him some records and a new stereo, and has Alex sign a document obviously releasing the present government from any responsibility concerning Alex. Alex, however, says he does "not know[ ] what I was signing, and [does] not, O my brothers, car[e] either" (178–79). In the final paragraph Alex gives himself over to Beethoven's Ninth Symphony and dreams of "carving the whole litso of the creeching world with my cut-throat britva." At the end of this story about education, Alex might or might not have learned anything. At the end of this story about free will, Alex might or might not still be a slave. At the end of this story about regeneration, the irony of the last line sounds loud and clear: "I was cured all right" (179).

If, on the other hand, the reader runs with what Burgess loadedly calls "the British or international" version (*Rolling Stone* 76) and finishes with the twenty-first chapter, he or she is liable to read from a closed, modern perspective. Seven chapters in each section adds up to twenty-one chapters in all, and for Burgess "the number twenty-one is the symbol of human maturity, or used to be, since at twenty-one you got the vote and assumed adult responsibility" (75–76). The number twenty-one, then, is the number of closure, completion, and wholeness. And it is in the twenty-first chapter that Alex, according to Burgess,

grows bored with violence and recognizes human energy is better expended on creation than destruction. Senseless violence is a prerogative of youth, which has much energy but little talent for the constructive. Its dynamism has to find an outlet in smashing telephone kiosks, derailing trains, stealing cars and smashing them and, of course, in the much more satisfactory activity of destroying human beings. There comes a time, however, when violence is seen as juvenile and boring. It is the repartee of the stupid and ignorant. My young hoodlum comes to the revelation of the need to get something done in life: to marry, to beget children, to keep the orange of the world turning in the rookers of Bog, or hands of God, and perhaps even create something—music, say. (76)

Following this reading, in chapter twenty-one the reader is supposed to believe that Alex can and does abruptly change. Without warning, he grows up. Alex and his three new droogs go to the Korova Milkbar in a scene that circles back to the first of the novel, thereby structurally affirming a sense of fulfillment. In the midst of their banter, Alex feels "both very tired and also full of tingly energy" (78). He needs to get out and so they decide to take a walk down Marghanita Boulevard. Alex watches rather than participates in the beating his droogs administer to an old man at a news kiosk. In the Duke of New York, a photograph of a baby Alex can't account for falls out of his pocket, and, embarrassed, he tears it up. He realizes as he does so, however, that it's really his droogs "who's the babies. . . . Scoffing and grinning and all [they] can do is smeck and give people bolshy cowardly tolchocks when they can't give them back" (76). Alex sets out a second time, now on his own, and in a tea-and-coffee shop he finds his old droog Pete sitting with his new wife. This pleasant scene shakes Alex, who sets out for a third time (the number three, of course, having both religious connotations and connotations of symmetry and closure). He sees visions of himself "coming home from work to a good hot plate of dinner, and there was this ptitsa all welcoming and greeting like loving" (76). It occurs to Alex that he is growing up: "Youth must go, ah yes. But youth is only being in a way like it might be an animal" (76). And with that Alex finishes his tale. At the end of *this* story about education, Alex has learned about adulthood. At the end of this story about free will, Alex has—if surely suddenly and somewhat melodramatically—chosen the Good. At the end of this story about regeneration, Alex has literally become a New Man.

Just the same, there is a second and more open way to read this last chapter. Certainly it is not a way Burgess intends, but it is a way the text clearly accepts. First, the sudden and melodramatic transformation on Alex's part, which takes much less than a chapter to run its course, is undercut by the highly skeptical comic tone of the preceding one hundred and seventy-nine pages and twenty chapters. After the reader has learned from Alex that one should not take anything too seriously and that solutions to complex problems are always much more complicated than they might at first seem, maybe even impossible, s/he has a hard time taking the last chapter at solemn face value. Second, though related, is the fact that Alex's last move is wholly out of character for him. The reader surely finds it difficult to swallow the idea that Alex has begun to become the very static bourgeois presence that he has scorned throughout the novel. Moreover, the metamorphosis into that static bourgeois presence has been set up only pages before it actually happens so that the change is far too abrupt to be convincing. Third, the ironic tone of the last paragraph ruptures the seemingly serious tone that came just before it:

> But where I itty now, O my brothers, is all on my oddy knocky, where you cannot go. Tomorrow is all like sweet flowers and the turning vonny earth and the stars and the old Luna up there and your old droog Alex all on his oddy knocky seeking like a mate. And all that cal. A terrible grahzny vonny world, really, O my brothers. And so farewell from your little droog. And to all others in this story profound shooms of lip-music brrrrrr. And they can kiss my sharries. But you, O my brothers, remember sometimes thy little Alex that was. Amen. And all that cal. (80)

At the same time Alex implicates the reader in his story with all three (again, the number three) uses of "O my brothers," he also distances himself from the reader for the first time, since he claims he is going "where you cannot go." In the same phrase, apparently an allusion to his entry into the adult world, he taunts and insults the reader: the suggestion is both that Alex won't tell us what comes next in his narrative (does this mean there is a chance he fails to become an "adult"?) and that the reader is too immature to enter the adult world with Alex. The next line holds within itself all the innocent lyricism of Scarlet O'Hara at the end of *Gone with the Wind,* but it is also disrupted by means of the brutal cynicism of the following line: "And all that cal." The optimism of "tomorrow is all like sweet flowers" topples on the bitter pessimism of "the turning vonny earth" and "a grahzny vonny world." Alex ends with "profound shooms of lip-music" to "all others in this story"; he gives the raspberries, that is, both to his adolescent droogs and to the complacent bourgeosie, to the prof types and to the millicents, to all forms of authority and to all forms of anarchy, to *all* the others in his story, telling them that "they can kiss my sharries." He ends with a last lyrical lament for his old self that he claims to have left behind ("But you, O my brothers, remember sometimes thy little Alex that was. Amen."), only to pull the rug out from under his sincerity once more by adding "And all that cal."

Alex's last word has nothing to do with the universe of religious epiphany and affirmation ("Amen") but with that of cynical scatology and decomposition ("cal"). The irony, then, goes a long way toward destabilizing the possible validity of Alex's transformation, and there is more than a suggestion that this last chapter becomes a kind of joke that old Alex plays on the unsuspecting reader who has been waiting all along for the compensation of traditional narrative in a wholly untraditional world. In this way Alex becomes a cousin of the archetypal comic hero, less concerned with controlling the universe than with making sure the universe doesn't control him. He becomes as well the great grandson of Duchamp, bringing into question the fundamental values of art while having a ball pulling the rug out from under himself and us, his dear readers.

Garden of Forking Paths

In Janus-texts such as *Lolita* and *A Clockwork Orange* we locate a narratological and metaphysical world in extremis. *Lolita* longs for the transcendental signified of art that will ultimately turn chaos into cosmos, while at the same time taking mischievous delight in McFate-Nabokov's deconstruction of all transcendental signifieds. To return to Pearce's observations for a moment, Nabokov's text has much to do with the Feast of Fools, that English New Year's revel that overturns traditional restraints and sets free a joyful demonic energy. "Creative vitality is achieved through the playful release of destructive energy, the diabolical thrill of turning life into a game, the comic urge toward disorder and nihilistic destruction," Pearce writes. "In the end the world is turned upside down, order is destroyed, reality is undermined by a comic force that is at once threatening and enlivening" (Cohen 30). *Lolita* ultimately is a text that desires modernity, but which subverts itself through a postmodern charge.

In the same way, *A Clockwork Orange* longs to be a modern satiric text in line with Orwells's *1984* and Huxley's *Brave New World* with all the possibility of a moral vision such a mode of discourse implies, but here satire is unsure of itself, unstable. In order to work, satire must assume an accepted set of communal values. Swift's "A Modest Proposal," for instance, is successful only to the extent that its audience believes it is wrong to kill children and make them into lampshades and gloves. A problem arises, though, when the audience is unsure of what it is supposed to believe. Often when freshmen misread the satiric irony of "A Modest Proposal," academics wring their hands and point toward one more example of the growing illiteracy sweeping our culture. Another way to view such a misreading, however, is to see it as a reflection of the inability of our postmodern culture to know what its values are. After all, in the aftermath of World War II, when in fact a portion of the global population *did* believe it right to kill children and turn them into lampshades and gloves, it becomes exceedingly difficult to locate a stable set of ethical values by which to read a text. We can't read a text as stable irony unless we know what we believe as a culture.

If we add to this Wayne Booth's observation that satiric irony becomes increasingly difficult to spot the more complexity, subtlety, and private norms a text evinces, it is even more difficult to decide how to read certain texts. Modern texts are the last to be more or less sure of their values and to project those values in such a way that they are fairly easy for a reader to retrieve. It is clear, for instance, that Eliot embraces the classical aesthetic values of the Great Tradition in *The Waste Land,* that Conrad embraces the humanist if racist values associated with Marlow rather than the antihumanist ones associated with Kurtz in *Heart of Darkness,* and that Sartre embraces the late humanist values of existentialism in *Nausea.*

Texts such as *A Clockwork Orange,* on the other hand, despite what their authors have to say about them, stutter on a continuum between the modern search for a moral vision and the postmodern delegitimation of all centers of authority, including morality. In a world where it is not apparently moral for an individual to dodge the draft or disrupt the placement of nuclear weapons in Europe but where it is apparently moral for companies to bury vast amounts of toxic waste near city water supplies and to produce weather systems of acid rain, books such as *Lolita* and *A Clockwork Orange* (as well as those diverse as Beckett's *Murphy,* Borges's "Library of Babel," Barth's *End of the Road,* Robbe-Grillet's *The Erasers,* and Vonnegut's *Slaughter-House Five*) transform into Janus-texts. They become desperate texts. They become, like Ts'ui Pên's novel described in Borges's parable of postmodern reading, a garden of forking paths where "all possible outcomes occur," where "each one is the point of departure for other forkings" (*Labyrinths* 26), and where the labyrinths go on forever.

IV
THE MINDCIRCUS
IN MOTION

5.
Postmodernism as Gag

deterioration of the sense of humour fewer
tears too that too they are failing too
—Beckett, *How It Is*

Statesmen and Dogshit

Beckett picks up where writers such as Nabokov and Burgess leave off. If satire in particular depends on the existence of a communal sense of moral values, then humor in general depends on the existence of a communal sense of reasonable behavior. For something to be funny, that thing has to deviate in some way from what we think of as the norm. A pompous statesman, for example, isn't very funny. A pompous statesman doing the fandango as he skids in a pile of dogshit *is*. Without a fairly stable definition of what constitutes the norm, humor becomes even more relative than usual, even more situation- and person-specific. In postmodern culture, as I have stressed throughout this book, our ideas of what constitutes the norm are assaulted every day. This is the culture in which housewives talk with their houseplants, scientists talk with their dolphins, and my less-than-reliable checkout-line tabloid tells the story of a woman who died from the rabies she received while attempting to give her pet bat, who had just had a tiny heart attack, mouth-to-mouth resuscitation.

It follows, as Earl Rovit argues, that "we can no longer count on a conditioned social or religious sense of decorum which will enable us to distinguish between those extreme events which may shock us into laughter, and those which should elicit from us emotional paralysis, disgust, or religious awe" (Cohen 240). Rovit recalls photos of monks setting themselves on fire, eliciting titters from some viewers, and suggests that such dramatists as Ionesco and Albee have paved the way for audiences to see *King Lear* and the crucifixion simply as instances of hip comedy. Certainly, some viewers of *Monty Python's Flying Circus,* Eddie Murphy's schticks, the film *Brazil,* Dennis Hopper's performance in *Blue Velvet,* or the various commercial manifestations of the Garbage-Pail Kids find themselves more baffled or even indignant than amused.

Once more, then, we see that postmodern existence has metamorphosed from the ironic into the humorous. Whereas humans once confronted a reality that was basically sincere, interpretable, and filled with indications of how it should be read, we now face an unreality that is disingenuous, against interpretation, and unreadable. Ironists perceive such a postmodern pluriverse as tragic because no truth is discoverable within it. Humorists perceive such a postmodern pluriverse as comic because no truth is discoverable within it. Texts produced by a humorous culture are of course themselves humorous, and the humorous text, as Lang acknowledges, "does not express meaning in the traditional, etymological sense of exteriorizing what was interior to the authorial psyche . . . ; it organizes a number of linguistic elements into systems offering a variety of potential meanings to be actualized by the reader" (6). It is designed to generate a multiplicity of meaning, a carnival of (anti)interpretation, a mindcircus in motion.

Such humorous texts may take innumerable forms. One cannot and should not attempt to establish an anatomy of the postmodern text, cataloguing the techniques, the forms, the menus—McHale's work notwithstanding. The shape will change from one text to another, from one micronarrative to another. What remains constant is the humorous vision generating that shape. One thinks of the multidimensional and mutually exclusive unrealities presented in Coover's "The Baby Sitter"; Sukenick's collage pages in *98.6;* Pynchon's verbal explosion in *Gravity's Rainbow;* Burrough's antilanguage in *Naked Lunch;* William Gibson's antiworlds in *Neuromancer, Count Zero,* and *Mona Lisa Overdrive;* Barthes's intellectual gymnastics in *S/Z;* Derrida's heteroglossia in *Glas.* In each case, the disruptions occur via different means, different designs, many of which may be shared with modern or even premodern texts. The constant is the obsession with comic disruption. The vision that produces the shape or seeming shapelessness has at least as much to do with the Keystone Kops, Keaton, and Duchamp as it does with such "weighty" ideas as the

End of Western Humanism, the Death of the Self, and the Pathos of
Contemporary Mankind. When a communal norm of reasonable behavior has broken down, all the rest is a matter of reading.

How It Is

William Gass told me that, when he teaches Beckett's *How It Is*
(French, 1961; English, 1964) in his course on literature and philosophy, his students complain relentlessly if he gives them a chance to.
So he doesn't give them a chance to. He continues to teach the book
for what he likes to think of as his students's own good. This jibes
weirdly well with my own experience of teaching *How It Is* in my
course on postmodern fiction. I have found it one of the most difficult
texts *to* teach, not only because that book (which took Beckett eighteen awful months to write) is so tricky to talk about, but also because
my students evince deep frustration generated from their inability to
figure out whether or not such a gruesome thing is actually supposed
to be funny.

I tell them that as much as Beckett is grounded in the heavy European tradition of Dante, Descartes, Geulincx, the French Symbolists,
and Proust, he is also grounded in the humorous Anglo-American
tradition of Swift, Sterne, Dickens, Joyce, and the Keystone Kops.
When he was a boy in Dublin, Beckett discovered slapstick and prat-
falls at the Queens Theatre, and he often attended vaudeville at the
Theatre Royal and the Olympia. He saw every film starring Charlie
Chaplin, Laurel and Hardy, Harold Lloyd, and the Marx Brothers.
He offered Buster Keaton the role of Lucky in the first American
production of *Waiting for Godot,* though Keaton turned it down. He
offered Keaton the role of O in *Film,* which Keaton accepted, although he confessed that he didn't know "what the hell was going on"
in it (Bair 574).

Shortly after completing *How It Is,* whose printer claimed it was
mere porno that ruined his eyes (Bair 524), Beckett asserted that
previous art had attempted creating cosmos out of chaos, "form" out
of "mess." What he intended to do, on the other hand, was to admit
the mess into his art because "we have come into a time when [the
mess] invades our experience at every moment. It is there and it must
be allowed in." "To find a form that accommodates the mess," he
added, "that is the task of the artist now" (Bair 523). Aesthetically,

Beckett's statement has much in common with Ronald Sukenick's Mosaic Law, the attempt to deal "with parts in the absence of wholes" (*98.6* 122), and with Lyotard's idea that postmodernism "denies itself the solace of good forms" and "searches for new presentations, not in order to enjoy them but in order to import a stronger sense of the unpresentable" (*Postmodern Condition* 81). Nathan Scott calls such projects examples of Hunger Art after the father of postmodernism's parable of self-denial. Hunger Art is that which repudiates frames of reference, subverts tradition, and refuses conclusion (*Negative Capability* 53–54).

By injecting mess into form, *How It Is* turns itself into a kind of gag played on the reader accustomed to conventional modern and pre-modern narratological and metaphysical strategies. Beckett originally intended to take the gag to an even greater extreme than he has by printing the text as one long paragraph unbroken by punctuation, capitalization, or typographical marks but apparently changed his mind after publishing a section of it in the journal *X* (Bair 521). Rather, he decided to divide the work into short unpunctuated prose-poems separated by white spaces that signal pauses for the breaths that the narrator must take on his unending crawl through an ocean of so-called mud, which may in fact be "nothing more than all our shit" (52)—if in fact there is a narrator, if in fact he is breathing, if in fact he is crawling through the mud, and if in fact that mud is excrement.

Early on, such suppositions begin to disintegrate as the voice speaking indicates that "YOU BOM me Bom ME BOM you Bom we Bom" (76), and that "Bem is therefore Bom or Bom Bem" (113). The suggestion is that "in reality we are one" (140), that all the "characters" in the text are simply various sides of one personality, one voice, but even this is brought into serious question when the reader is told "and no again I'm sorry again no one here knows himself it's the place without knowledge" (123). In the trilogy the reader watches the self decompose from one, through the fractions, toward zero, from Molloy, Moran, Malone, MacMann, and Mahood to Basil, Worm, and finally the Unnamable, so that in the end there is nothing but a discharge of prose on the page, collapsed syntax and tense, unsure gender and subject. What is left after the Unnamable is how it is—a consciousness (?) that knows nothing including itself. Perhaps it is hallucinating, perhaps stuck in a perpetual hypnagogic state. In any case, it generates an outpouring of garbled pseudosentences that run messily down the page while it hovers in a state of radical narrative and metaphysical uncertainty.

To put it another way, the reader can speak of the text only in a series of possibilities and tentative suggestions. Apparently, the one fact s/he can be sure of is that the subject is crawling (or thinks it is crawling) through the vast stretches of mud in the darkness, advancing minimally and resting, moving "say forty yards a year" (125)—though there is an indication that even that is an illusion (144) and though "how I got here no question not known not said" (7). If the reader is to take the image of crawling through mud and darkness as fact, then s/he is confronted by a mental picture reminiscent of Beckett and Suzanne's horrible night trek to Rousillon during their escape from the Gestapo in 1942. The reader might also be faced by some postnuclear future, as in *Endgame,* since we are told "but progress properly so called ruins in prospect as in the dear tenth century the dear twentieth that you might say to yourself to a dream greenhorn ah if you had seen it four hundred years ago what upheavals" (22). Or the reader might encounter some Dantean hell where the cursed subject dreams of the days "above in the light" (37) or by some Dantean purgatory where the cursed subject claims, "I don't drink any more and I don't eat any more don't move any more and don't sleep any more don't see anything any more and don't do anything any more" (40).

There is a hint of the Beckettian protagonist in his purest form, one whose first traces stretch back at least to the short story collection *More Pricks than Kicks* and Belacqua Shuah, whose name Beckett finds in the *Purgatorio* (iv, 97–135) and uses here (24). Belacqua is notorious for his laziness and apathy, having to wait in the shadow of a rock until as many years have passed as he lived on Earth. In Sandro Botticelli's illustration of Belacqua, of which Beckett makes several mentions in his early fiction and poetry, the embodiment of sloth sits in the fetal position in the shadow of his rock and "becomes an emblem of embryonic recoil from life and wearisome ascent" (McMillan 32).

The protagonist of *How It Is,* though not in the fetal position, does seem to move through a dark and primeval womblike world. He has recoiled from life above, or has been exiled from it, and what at first strikes the reader as strange about all this is that the subject's reaction to his unfastened and sometimes even violent environment is not one of rebellion or despair, but of assent and even contentment—one in which he "never disapprove[s of] anything really" (41). Supporting this view J. E. Dearlove makes the point that *How It Is* is not just one more rehearsal of the techniques and concerns found in the trilogy. "Instead," Dearlove notes, "the book marks a turning point in Samuel Beckett's career from an exploration of the limitations of the human mind and an emphasis upon definitions of self, to an identification of the self with the voice and an acceptance, if not a celebration, of the life of the imagination" (150). Utterly flexible, the subject takes the universe and its injustice as it comes to him and recalls the final words spoken by the Unnamable when he says "one can't go on one goes on as before can one ever stop put a stop that's more like it one can't go on one can't stop put a stop" (90). The reader uncovers the fictional emblem of Alan Wilde's postmodern person who "abandons the quest for paradise altogether" and accepts randomness and contingency as the stuff of life. Hope takes the form of "small satisfactions," as Stanley Elkin has said (qtd. by Wilde, 10). Here is the pure postmodern comic protagonist.

He gets along without much struggle and without much despair. He passes his time while crawling through the mud and the darkness by turning his imagination into a playground of the mind. He drifts into memories or daydreams having to do with lost love, falling, and death. In his mind's eye, he sees an anxious woman in the world of light stitching while the narrator, perhaps a boy, sits with his head resting on a table (10–11); a photo of a child kneeling and praying before its strict mother on a sunny veranda (15–16); the sixteen-year-old narrator walking a dog with his girlfriend on a lovely spring day (29); a young boy meeting Jesus (45); the narrator's wife Pam Prim shaving her pubic area and then jumping or falling from a window (76–77); his father comically toppling off scaffolding and landing on his arse (78); and his genital licking dog Skom Skum run over by a dray (85). Though it comes up, religion offers little by way of hope or pastime on the subject's grail-less quest, which he has a "strong feeling" is "from west to east" (40). Religion is neither significant nor absurd; its language is composed of vacant signifiers without signifieds, since "the belief the blue the miracles all lost never was" (70).

Instead, the subject passes time examining his hand, which is "a resource when all fails" (14), intricately concerning himself with the most comfortable position for sleep (24), which affords him half-hour (19) intervals of peace and quiet, lapping the mud because that "lasts a good moment they are good moments perhaps the best difficult to choose" (27), and, like Watt and the narrator of *The Lost Ones,* doing his math in order to bring some certainty to all this confusion. "I always loved arithmetic it has paid me back in full" (37), the subject claims, and it appears that the more complicated the calculations are the more pleasure he finds in this "serious effort of the imagination":

as for example our course a closed curve and let us be numbered 1 to 1000000 then number 1000000 on leaving his tormentor number 999999

instead of launching forth into the wilderness towards an inexistent
victim proceeds towards number 1

and number 1 forsaken by his victim number 2 does not remain eter-
nally bereft of tormentor since this latter as we have seen in the person
of number 1000000 is approaching with all the speed he can muster
right leg right arm push pull ten yards fifteen yards

and three if only three of us and so numbered only 1 to 3 four rather it's
preferable clearer picture if only four of us and so numbered only 1 to 4

then two places only at the extremities of the greatest chord say A and
B the four couples the four abandoned two tracks only of a semi-orbit
each say how shall we say AB and BA for the travellers (117–18)

Beings are abstracted into numbers, and numbers skedaddle up and
down the page, the "narrator's" mind doing a metaphysical vaudeville routine of Who's On First. The point is not so much following
the knotty permutations of the mathematics as enjoying the numbers-
as-clowns bumping into and tripping over each other, accepting if not
celebrating the ongoing circus of the imagination that makes the only
sense of the world it knows how to—a kind of sense, ultimately, that
is really not so different from a kind of nonsense, a megalithic and
probably untrue pattern of sadomasochism.

In this pattern, mathematical symmetry must be maintained. Every victimizer must also be victim. Like a vision of Nietzschean eternal recurrence, "we pass the two kinds of solitude the two kinds of
company through which tormenters abandoned victims travellers we
all pass and pass again being regulated thus are of equal duration"
(125). The text itself is symmetrical, written in three equal parts
representing the time before Pim, during Pim, and after Pim. The
relationship between the subject and Pim seems equally divided between something like harmony and harshness. At times the protagonist hoists himself up so he can touch Pim's old and bearded face, and
something very near love, surely basic human need, asserts itself: "in
the dark the mud my head against his my side glued to his my right
arm round his shoulders his cries have ceased we lie thus a good
moment they are good moments" (54). But at times, too, comes the
subject's grotesquely humorous and sadistic behaviorist regimen reminiscent of that perpetrated by the state in *A Clockwork Orange*:
"table of basic stimuli one sing nails in armpit two speak blade in arse
three stop thump on skull four louder pestle on kidney" (69). Com-
panionship for the protagonist is divided between these two poles of

97

tenderness and brutality. It may appear a sad state of affairs to the modern ironic reader, but to the humorous postmodern protagonist it is simply how it is. "I'll never let it go call that constancy if you wish" (55), he says, though, clearly, he does let it go and imagines that he enters the pattern again, ending as a traveller waiting to have his turn as victim.

Chances might be, however, that he doesn't enter the pattern again, that there never was any Pim separate from his own mind, that the subject has only had his consciousness with which to toy, perhaps his own body. This might account for his frequent focus on scatology. Such detailed representation of bodily functions as appear in *How It Is* stands for dark mirth at man's irrational half, an extreme parody of the mimetic impulse in the arts, a perverse parody of Freudian-Darwinian consciousness. At the same time that it signals a drive toward the extension of the self in the universe, it also signals the desecration of humanist environments—high art, bourgeois decorum, the body itself, the religious artifact. Moreover, for the protagonist, scatology and reason are linked: "the great needs fail the need to move on the need to shit and vomit and the other great needs all my great categories of being" (14). Categories of being are linked with shit and vomit. Philosophy—human thought—is linked with scatology. Scatology is equated with speech itself: "I strain with open mouth so as not to lose a second a fart fraught with meaning issuing through the mouth" (26). The very act of communication is decomposed to the level of a quiet breaking of wind, a sound just this side of silence, a postmodern whoopie cushion.

The words on the page also take on a scatological appearance, running messily down before the reader, refusing the retentive order of punctuation, capitals, and traditional paragraphing. This nonarrangement coupled with Beckett's frequent and innovative use of white space, acknowledges what Sukenick calls the "technological reality" of the text. Sukenick believes we have to "learn how to look at fiction as lines of print on a page," "have to learn to think about a novel as a concrete structure rather than an allegory" (206). Realist fiction, of course, treats the novel as allegory. In it, fiction is treated as fact; words on the page are a gateway to reality. Beckett—as well as other postmodern humorists such as Federman with his use of concrete poetry in *Double or Nothing,* Vonnegut with his use of scribbles in *Breakfast of Champions,* and Mas'ud Zavarzadeh with his use of pastiche in "The Critic as Riot Police: Readerly Criticism and Receivable Fictions"—short-circuits such as innocent enterprise by foregrounding the physicality of the text in the reader's hands.

Whereas realist fiction neutralizes words, postmodern humorous fiction exploits their appearance on the page, jamming progress in the
fictional world and underscoring the reader's position in real time.
So, in *How It Is* at least two universes are in continual battle: the
vague amorphous one of the protagonist and the nitty-gritty real one
of the reader. As a result, the very act of reading paradoxically helps
in the decomposition of the protagonist, who gains existence only
through being read.

Alongside or behind or above or within this protagonist there apparently exists another voice—a muse, perhaps, or a divinity, or several beings at once, though the subject comments that "who is speaking that's not said any more it must have ceased to be of interest"
(21). This secondary subject tries to communicate through the primary subject, but, comically, the primary subject can't clearly hear
what he's being told. He might "say it as [he] hear[s] it," but what he
hears is "ill-said ill-heard ill-recaptured ill-murmured," and there are
"losses everywhere" (7). He might be playing a game of telephone
with God Himself, but the only message he gets is a pastiche of "bits
and scraps barely audible . . . so little so faint not the millionth part"
(15), and "it starts so sudden comes so faint goes so fast ends so soon
I'm on it in a flash it's over" (81). Sometimes he believes that there is
a source but the "words won't come," and sometimes he begins to
worry that maybe he isn't really hearing anything at all. "It's one or
the other," he says, accepting to the end, and this ambiguous realization makes him "a little happy on and off" (18). The secondary subject might also be Beckett himself, trying to instill some meaning in
his protagonist, trying to stabilize the fictional world, a Wizard of Oz
behind his curtain. If this is the case, however, the poor wizard flick-
ers in and out of existence just as his characters do, neither wholly
present nor wholly absent.

The reader is left, then, with uncertain place, uncertain time, uncertain characters, and uncertain events, all of which are expressed "unbroken no paragraphs not a second for reflection" (70), perhaps one
more version of "all our shit" (52), one more scatological outpouring,
language half-digested and expelled. The ignorance and impotence of
this verbiage not only undoes the well-made sentence of the realist
tradition but dismantles the energetic Joycean sentence that believed
in the omnipotence and omnipresence of art. While the Joycean sentence concerned itself with creation (art-as-redeemer, the quest toward surreality through the window of epiphany), the Beckettian sentence concerns itself with entropy (art-as-deconstructor, the quest
toward minimalism through the window of exhaustion). Beckett does

not give the reader story but discourse, and the discourse lacks much imagery, metaphor or splendor. It is pared down to surfaces. Its content and its form come apart in the reader's hands.

All the reader is finally left with is a series of epistemological and ontological questions: What is there to know? How can I know it? What are the limits of the knowable? To what extent can one know something? What kind of existence is this? Is this how it is? Who is in this world? What is a self? What is a human? What is living? What is life?

How It Isn't, or: The Gag

The ultimate gag, then, does not come at the level of the subject, a bumbling sometimes happy antiheroic Keatonesque clown who lives in "quasi-certitude" and who "always understood everything except for example history and geography" (41)—everything, that is, except when he is and where, and, by implication, how he got there and why.

Instead, the ultimate gag occurs at the level of text itself. As readers, we must soon grant that we don't exactly know what's happening, or where it's happening, or to whom it's happening. In addition, we continually struggle to find out what isn't happening by reading a nonlanguage that often collapses before it has yielded up much, if any, sense. We either fail in our reading project or learn to be as flexible in the face of textual contingency and injustice as the protagonist must learn to be in the face of cosmic contingency and injustice. In quasi-certitude we contentedly hold up a few facts as the subject does his sack of goodies and we exclaim that we have made some meaning in this narratological universe because we have been taught that that is what stories should do—make sense of things, find things out, put things in some kind of order—and because we have been taught that that is what critics should do. We read ironically and become frustrated because we cannot find the message darkly concealed beneath the surface of the text, and hence we come to feel that because the text is meaningless it must also be worthless. Or we learn to read humorously, as the protagonist reads his universe, and we find a few good moments and guard them anxiously.

But even as we are deciding how to read this text, the final scaffolding is jerked out from under us as from under the subject's father. Beckett, we learn, refuses to satisfy even our elementary needs. The last shreds of the definite are taken away from us, and we tumble off our structure of reason and land on our arses. As we round the homestretch of text, only three pages to the end, happy on and off that we have uncovered at least the remnants of patterns in a seemingly patternless universe, the subject announces that we haven't been in a race, haven't been riding a horse, and look fairly silly sitting in the dirt striking the ground with our crop: "all these calculations yes explanations yes the whole story from beginning to end yes completely false yes." Everything we have been told, everything we have struggled over, we are now informed, has been a lie, a fiction, a prank. We learn "that wasn't how it was no not at all no how then no answer." Perhaps we have discovered something, though Lord knows what. We most certainly haven't discovered how it is. "There was something," the subject slyly states, "but not of all that." In fact, "this voice quaqua yes all balls yes only one voice yes mine yes when the panting stops yes" (144–45). We do the fandango as we skid on the pile of postmodernism:

> yes never any procession no nor any journey no never any Pim no nor any Bom no never anyone no only me no answer only me yes so that was true yes it was true about me yes and what's my name no answer WHAT'S MY NAME screams good (146)

We are given one last straw to clutch, however, when we are told that it was "only me in any case yes alone yes in the mud yes the dark yes that holds" (146). But *does* it hold? We have just been told that everything has been untrue. Now we are told that not everything we have been told has been untrue. We find ourselves squarely set in the midst of Eubulides' paradox. A man has just told us that he is lying. Now, is what he says true or false? Is the liar who tells us he is lying, though not entirely, lying or not entirely lying? The answer is, as the subject makes his refrain in the penultimate prose-poem, that there is "no answer" (147). How it is is that we shall never know how it is.

Everybody's Doin' It

Richard Chase in his cornerstone study of American literature argues that the American novel "tends to rest in contradictions and among extreme ranges of experience" (1) whereas the British novel "is notable for its practical sanity, its powerful, engrossing composition of wide ranges of experience into a moral centrality and equability of judgment" (2). As I hope I have just demonstrated, though, nothing could be farther from fact. Surely, Beckett's book is as wholly uninterested in pragmatism, wide ranges of experience, morality, and judgment as those by Alan Singer, Thomas Berger, and Richard Brautigan—let alone such non–Anglo-American writers as Italo Calvino, Peter Handke, and Hélène Cixous.

My point, of course, is not to conclude that Chase's valuable argument is incorrect, only that his critical study is the product and register of a modern ironic sensibility that might help shed some light on the postmodern humorous one. Since he made his observations back in 1957 (about, I should add, a period of literature that extended from 1798 and *Wieland* to 1932 and *Light in August*) postmodernism has come into dominance and our culture has come to conceive of itself as hypercosmopolitan. We can fly from New York to London in a few hours and from Earth to the moon in a few days. We can buy Coke in Bejing and García Márquez's latest novel, translated into English, in our local bookstores the same moment it appears in Latin American ones. Satellites have linked the world in such a way that a whole generation of kids, including myself, grew up sitting at the dinner table in various towns across the United States, watching teenagers die in Vietnamese rice patties. That our planet has shrunk to a global village has become a chic cliché, and the essence of a cliché, we should remember, is its pith of truth.

The pith of truth here is that boundaries between different cultures have begun to erode. Cultural identities have begun to be neutralized. Postmodernity perceives itself as a transnational and transcultural mode that has cropped up in countries as different as England and Mexico, Canada and South Africa, and in artifacts as different as the novel and sculpture, rock 'n' roll and ballet. Contrary, then, to the implications of critics such as Wilde and Huyssen, who see postmodernity as primarily an American mode of consciousness, I maintain that by definition it is global in nature. It appears in work by writers as different as Christa Wolf and Angela Carter, Günter Grass and Alain Robbe-Grillet, and Carlos Fuentes and Milan Kundera.

This development translates into the observation that the study of literature from a culturally specific vantage point (American Studies, for instance, or Latin American literature) has become a marvelously myopic practice, a thing of the past. Thirty years ago one could make the kind of distinctions Chase is interested in and be fairly confident of their applicability. Today the study of literature, of any artifact, requires that such artificial walls—between country and country, between discipline and discipline—come down as simply one more example of pomposity and rigidity, one more ironic target of the humorous mind. For the postmodern, the study of all cultural artifacts has become more comparative and less defined than ever before, and for the postmodern this means a heaven of heterotopias.

6.
Linguistic Pratfalls

Why does language subvert me, subvert my
seniority, my medals, my oldness, whenever
it gets a chance? What does language have
against me—me that has been good to it,
respecting its little peculiarities and
nicilosities, for sixty years.
—Donald Barthelme, *Unspeakable Practices*

Heteroglossia

A critical commonplace: absurdity, parody, irony, burlesque, farce, and satire abound at the stratum of events in Donald Barthelme's projects. In "The Joker's Greatest Triumph," a spoof on our superchic cartoonish consumer society, for instance, Batman is stunned and finally unmasked while his friend—or perhaps lover?—Fredric Brown looks on horrified, and Robin, who is supposed to be away at Andover doing poorly in French, swoops out of the Gotham City sky in a backup Batplane as a kind of comic-book *deus ex machina*. Conscious again, our superhero undertakes a textual analysis of the arch villain by paraphrasing Mark Schorer's biography of Sinclair Lewis.

Another critical commonplace: often the fantastic mislocation of events in Barthelme's fictions is overshadowed by the discourse that shapes it. In fact, it is not infrequently that nothing much happens in his works. Two people sit in an underground missile silo and watch each other in "Game." A doctor contemplates his best friend's wife while spinning on a piano stool in "Alice." A ludicrous lyrical philosopher contemplates existential absence for four pages in "Nothing: A Preliminary Account." One is reminded of Herbert Blau's assertion that "when what you're doing isn't either necessary or probable, it is inevitably comic" (20).

Since the middle of the 1970s Barthelme has constituted his pieces more and more out of pure dialogue devoid of traditional tags that let us know who is speaking, and where, and why, thereby undercutting the Balzacian mode of fiction. Barthelme's pieces point to themselves as artificial and deliberate modes of discourse and flag their self-reflexivity, joining works by writers such as Butor in France, Cabrera Infante in Cuba and then England, and Gaddis in the United States. Interest, then, falls on the signifier and its relationship both to the writer and reader. Interest falls on the linguistic game in the texts, the lexical play on the page.

What is *not* a critical commonplace is that such verbal frolic in Barthelme's projects carries with it affinities to the cinematic slapstick of Chaplin, Laurel and Hardy, Keaton, and others. Though I should not want to suggest a simple cause-and-effect relationship between Barthelme's film interests and his fiction, I should want to point out that Barthelme is well acquainted with the knockabout falls and fast-speed chases that were the mainstay of comic films from 1912 onward. As a child growing up in Texas, he attended movies habitually. As the editor of *Cougar,* the college newspaper at the University of Houston, he reviewed films in 1950 and 1951. When he turned reporter for the *Houston Post,* he reviewed a wide range of cultural events, including cinematic ones. Since the middle of the 1960s, he has turned out a number of essays on the current cinema for the *New Yorker.* He has also acknowledged the profound effect film has had on contemporary consciousness and has suggested a link between film and fiction generally. Just as modern painters had to reinvent painting because of the discovery of photography, he has argued, so contemporary writers have had to reinvent writing because of the discovery of film—which, I assume, has to do with both the new subject matter and the fragmentary, short-scened, high-paced, surface-oriented form ("Symposium on Fiction" 26). (It is well known that Barthelme eschews the term *postmodern,* although William Gass has told me Barthelme also hosts an annual parodic party for the postmoderns.)

What is important in Barthelme's projects, however, is that the situational has transfigured into the discursive. Sight gags have metamorphosed into language gags. Following Frederik N. Smith's approach in "Beckett's Verbal Slapstick," I should like to suggest that

Barthelme takes the dislocation that is, according to Kant, Schopenhauer, Freud, and Bergson, at the core of comedy, plucks it out of the domain of events and plugs it into the domain of discourse. He presents the reader with the knockabout falls and futile chases of a language trying to remain on its own two feet and catch up with some kind of steady, clear meaning. His language wears outrageously ill-fitting words that bump and thump over themselves, in ineffectual pursuit of a center, careering off cliffs of significance into ridiculousness. As a result, a brand of linguistic illegality arises. The dogma of lexical and tonal consistency collapses. Verbal banana peels undermine the self-confident syntax of an earlier mode of writing and slip up the tidy control every sentence once wanted over itself.

To accomplish this, Barthelme often plays around with what the structuralists and Barthelme himself in *Snow White* (44) call "universes of discourse"—areas of vocabulary, as Stephen Ullmann argues, which "fits together and delimit each other like pieces in a mosaic. In each field some sphere of experience is analyzed, divided up and classified in a unique way" (12). Rather than interesting himself in consistent universes of discourse—as did moderns such as Mann, Proust, and Conrad to some extent and the so-called realists such as Flaubert, George Eliot, and Tolstoy—Barthelme concerns himself with stylistic deformity and the inherent incongruities of language it assumes. Thus, he sets up one sector of vocabulary (thereby generating certain reader expectations about the linguistic unit's level of usage, social register, inflection, and so on) only immediately to insert another or several others (and shattering those expectations). Consequently, the original sector of vocabulary takes a dive.

If Foucault speaks of a text in which worlds come together and clash as a heterotopia, then, perhaps we can speak of a text in which discourses come together and clash as a *heteroglossia,* as McHale suggests (166). A heteroglossia is the linguistic equivalent of pastiche. That is, if pastiche occurs in a three-dimensional reality of sculpture, architecture, and performance, then heteroglossia occurs in a two-dimensional reality of the written text. Heteroglossia slams together different universes of discourse within a single text in an attempt to carnivalize language, to generate a funhouse of a polyphonic, indecorous, disrupted text that refuses a monologic vision. We are back to Bakhtin here, and back to Menippean satire, which blends various mutually exclusive types of discourse together in an extended mode of interrogation that has little concern for answer and much concern for process. Or, as Barthelme's protagonist in "Nothing: A Preliminary Account" claims at the end of a futile four pages of trying to pin down the nature of existential absence: "What a wonderful list! How joyous the notion that, try as we may, we cannot do other than fail and fail absolutely and that the task will remain always before us, like a meaning for our lives" (*Sixty Stories* 248). The process of interrogation, clearly, *isn't* a meaning, if by a meaning one imagines an absolute sense of truth. Rather, it is only *like* a meaning since it gives one something to do, gives direction to one's life. Of course, here what one *does* is fail. But, given the essence of postmodern acceptance, failure can be wonderful too. Failure only turns into ironic tragedy when one plays a game whose goal is to reach the safety zone of meaning. If, on the other hand, the goal of the game is simply playing the game, then failure to reach the safety zone in fact signals the game's success.

Peculiarities and Nicilosities

Examples of heteroglossia in Barthelme occur at all linguistic strata from the sentence to the text as a whole (as they do in works by other postmodern humorists such as Nabokov in *Pale Fire,* Barth in *Letters,* Cortázar in *Hopscotch,* Lessing in *Briefing for a Descent into Hell,* and Derrida in *Glas*). To begin small and subtle, let us look at an instance from one of Barthelme's best-known and frequently anthologized fictions, "The Glass Mountain" (based on the fairy tale "The Princess on the Glass Hill"): "The sidewalks were full of dogshit in brilliant colors: ocher, umber, Mars yellow, sienna, viridian, ivory black, rose madder" (*Sixty Stories* 179). The verbal *splat!,* to use Smith's metaphor, takes place as the text brings together the word *dogshit* (from the universe of discourse of street talk) with the lyrical and precise list of "brilliant colors" (from the lexical field of the eloquent artist). The prosaic with its two hard syllables topples the poetic with its exquisite cluster of diverse and pleasingly smooth sounds: *o*-cher, *bur*-nt *um*-ber, *Mars yel-low, si-en-na, viri*-dian, i-*vory bla*-ck, *rose ma*-dder. Soon it becomes apparent that the sentence is not about the description of *feces,* but about the *description* of feces. In other words, it is a sentence about sentences, about writing, creating art. In the larger story, where the poetic of the fairy-tale genre slips on the prosaic—corpse piles, drug addicts shooting up in doorways, endlessly unfulfilled desire—the artist climbs toward a transcendental signified and the final realization that reaching such an absolute is never "plausible, not at all, not for a moment" (182).

A more pronounced pratfall occurs in "Alice," the internal record of an obstetrician's longing for his best friend's wife: "I want to fornicate with Alice but it is a doomed project fornicating with Alice there are obstacles impediments preclusions estoppels I will exhaust them for you what a gas cruel deprivements SECTION SEVEN moral ambiguities SECTION NINETEEN Alice's thighs are like SECTION TWENTY-ONE " (69). This is a Beckettian "sentence," reminiscent of those in *How It Is*—and Barthelme is always nodding in the Irishman's direction—a clump of words whose pacing is jagged and clunky. Because of its lack of punctuation, it is in its very structure a sentence prone to trip over its own feet, "a doomed project." On top of this, it destroys any momentum it might have gained by switching universes of discourse three-fourths of the way through. Words like *fornicate, project, impediments, preclusions,* and *estoppels* are from the linguistic field of law. They possess an exact and unemotional charge. But as the sentence turns into the homestretch, it hits a linguistic banana peel, a unit from another universe. "What a gas" overthrows the authority of the first three-fourths of the sentence and sends it into a messy skid where it does a comic soft-shoe between the language of desire and legalese: "cruel" / "deprivements"; "Alice's thighs are like" / "SECTION TWENTY-ONE." Incongruity wells up as the dogma of the litigious factual tone, another kind of absolutism, skids on the perplexity of longing.

The same sort of interplay takes place at the level of paragraph and even passage, as in the following from *The Dead Father* (19):

> The Dead Father was slaying, in a grove of music and musicians. First he slew a harpist and than a performer upon the serpent and also a banger upon the rattle and also a blower of the Persian trumpet and one upon the Indian trumpet and one upon the Hebrew trumpet and one upon the Roman trumpet and one upon the Chinese trumpet of copper-covered wood. . . . and during a rest period he slew four buzzers and a shawmist and one blower upon the water jar . . . and then whanging his sword this way and that the Dead Father slew a cittern plucker . . . and two score of finger cymbal clinkers . . . and a sansa pusher and a manipulator of the guilded ball.
>
> The Dead Father resting with his two hands on the hilt of his sword, which was planted in the red and steaming earth.
>
> My anger, he said proudly.
>
> Then the Dead Father sheathing his sword pulled from his trousers his ancient prick and pissed upon the dead artists, severally and together, to the best of his ability—four minites, or one pint.

At the outset the tone of the passage is biblical. The repetition of the "he slew" and "upon the" formula echoes the universe of epic catalogues. "Hilt of his sword," "planted in the red and steaming earth," "my anger, he said," "sheathing his sword," and "severally and together" all cue the reader to expect the more elevated language of heroic legend whose center is a figure of imposing stature. But long before the end of the first passage, a hint ("whanging," "clinkers") appears that the conventional contract between reader and writer may be tenuous at best. Verbal slapstick sounds through loud and clear with the introduction of "prick," "pissed," and "four minutes, or one pint"—all from the universe of contemporary slang. The verbal planes shift, teeter, and tumble. Just as one of the impulses of the text as a whole is humorously to subvert traditional notions of the quest and romance by implanting them with anachronisms, characters that are difficult to distinguish, structures from painting, theater, and cartoons, the language of the text subverts traditional notions of the quest and romance by implanting them with a plethora of lexical fields that refuse the gravity of such traditional ideal visions. The only real quest here seems to be for different forms of linguistic frolic, different ways of making language career off the cliff.

A second instance of how this slapstick language works at the level of passage appears in "A Shower of Gold" (*Sixty Stories* 17), the story of Peterson, a sculptor who lives in a hypereducated age and who decides to go on a television program called "Who Am I?" to earn some extra money. Here his barber and lay analyst, Kitchen, talks about Peterson's relationship to the president, who has just burst into the sculptor's apartment and beaten him up:

> It's essentially a kind of I-Thou relationship, if you know what I mean. You got to handle it with full awareness of its implications. In the end one experiences only oneself, Nietzsche said. When you're angry with the President, what you experience is self-as-angry-with-the-President. When things are okay between you and him, what you experience is self-as-swinging-with-the-President. Well and good. *But* . . . you want the relationship to be such that what you experience is the-President-as-swinging-with-you. You want *his* reality, get it? So that you can break out of the hell of solipsism. How about a little more off the sides?

Peterson's is the story about how television has become *the* contemporary art form—a form that smashes us with thousands of information bits every evening, all popularized and anesthetized, so that in the end our consciousness is shaped by them; one ad on MTV tells us that this musical entertainment channel "is for the way you think." In a similar way, the above passage becomes a microcosm of the text. A number of lexical fields struggle and stumble over each other: psychology ("handle it," "full awareness of the implications"), philosophy ("I-Thou relationship," "one experiences only oneself," "hell of solipsism"), breezy hip American ("a kind of," "if you know what I mean," "you got to," "things are okay," "self-as-swinging-with-the-President," "well and good"), and even the language of barbershops ("a little more off the sides"). Freud, Buber, Sartre, and Nietzsche slide on the banana peel of a hip haircutter. The languages of psychology and philosophy are reduced to the level of psychobabble of the jazz musician and the barber (or is it the other way around?).

Snow White and *The Dead Father* generate the same kind of discursive clash, only this time it not only occurs at the strata of sentence and passage but at that of the text as a whole. Both projects are collage novels, texts constructed from fragments. The essence of the fragmentary form is mutilation, a sign of impossibility, jammed expectations, narrative incongruity. Mutilation is an essence of the postmodern, comic or not. For this reason, it is interesting that Barthelme, like Kafka, Borges, Robbe-Grillet, Cortázar, and a great number of other postmodern writers, finds it inconceivable to produce extended unified fictions that through their structure try to persuade us our lives are parts of an interlocking, beautifully sculpted whole. Kafka, in many ways the father of postmodernity in the twentieth century, could not complete any of the novels he began. Borges turned out short stories exclusively. The scant length of Robbe-Grillet's works is achieved only through the frequent repetition of a few scenes. Cortázar wrote a book called *Hopscotch* whose small parts one can literally shuffle around as one chooses. Barthelme fashions only short "stories" and defaced "novels."

In *Snow White* the reader comes upon a multitude of lexical fields bumbling into each other. The discursive universes of social science, philosophy, business, technology, politics, academics, and advertising misstep on those of comic books, television cartoons, hip lingo, film, songs, and fairy tales. In addition to most of these, *The Dead Father* includes the discursive universes from medicine, engineering, the thesaurus, the Bible, cliché, logic, mathematics, Lucky's speech in *Waiting for Godot,* romance, epic, and the how-to manual. Just as Snow White à la Barthelme finds it impossible to devise a steady and coherent identity for herself, since for her existence is an uninterpretable and inadequate script, so too the text finds it impossible to commit to a steady and coherent genre or language. The same is true of the

Dead Father, who has so many identities in the end he has none. He is both alive and dead, both mythic and comic, an omnipresent authority and a dismembered god, omnipotent and finally impotent. He is Orpheus, Zeus, Prometheus, Oedipus, Lear, and the Fisher King. Again, his personality is that of the text itself; both struggle for a pure literary identity only to be bulldozed into rubble.

Lyotard would say that both protagonist and text exist in a purely pagan postmodern state where there exist only micronarratives. The "rule" for both seems to be that one must "maximize as much as possible the multiplication of small narratives" (*Just Gaming* 59). And one must do this "without privileging any of them, without saying: This is a good one" (62).

Proliferating Possibilities

Such discursive slapstick has several functions. First, it undermines the stability of language itself. The power of words to mean falls under erasure, marking the moment of radical skepticism in Western culture Derrida points to when language itself is "invaded by the universal problematic; that in which, in absence of a center or origin, everything became discourse . . . when everything became a system where the central signified, the original or transcendental signified, is never absolutely present outside a system of differences. The absence of the transcendental signified extends the domain and interplay of signification *ad infinitum*" ("Structure, Sign, Play" 249). Language turns relative. Unfixed, it drifts among a multiplicity of "meanings." Any attempt at a stable linguistic "significance" decomposes into an infinite freeplay that refuses truth. Barthelme's pieces realize, as does the narrator of "Me and Miss Mandible," that "signs are signs, and some of them are lies" (*Sixty Stories* 34). Because one does not know which are *not* lies, it follows that, as Peterson in "A Shower of Gold" knows, "possibilities . . . proliferate and escalate all around us" (*Sixty Stories* 22).

The reader is asked to become partial prevaricator of the texts s/he reads, asked to frolic in intertextuality where, as Snow White knows, "my nourishment is refined from the ongoing circus of the mind in motion. Give me the odd linguistic trip, stutter and fall, and I will be content" (139). All one has left is the odd linguistic trip, stutter and fall, the trope, the surface of signifiers that have no absolute signifieds— language doing its tricks. One can play and enjoy the game. One can try to figure out all the rules. But one must also know at some level that the essence of any game is essentially gratuitous, that it creates only limited "meaning" in a limited environment, and that such "meaning" is only relative to the game itself and not to anything outside the game.

Moreover, the existence of discursive slapstick in the texts not only interrogates our notions of language, but it also interrogates that to which the words try to point—our world, our culture. With respect to this, Leonard Lutwack in his discussion of the form of the novel distinguishes between two modes of presentation in fiction: uniform style and mixed style. Texts employing the former—Lutwack cites *Pamela* and *The Ambassadors* as examples—signal the presence of a writer's conviction about a single, unambiguous, coherent view of reality. Lutwack writes: "A uniform style is assimilative in that it helps to create under a single aspect of language a single vision of the multiplicity of reality; it is a bond between author and reader, insuring that no different adjustment to language and viewpoint will be demanded from the reader than that established at the outset" (218). On the other hand, texts that employ a mixed style—*Moby Dick, Tristram Shandy, Gravity's Rainbow,* and Barthelme's pieces, for instance—signal a writer's *lack* of conviction about a single, unambiguous, coherent view of reality. Indeed, a mixed style might signal a writer who *revels* in refusing a compensatory and stable vision. It might revel in multiplicity. Again, Lutwack: "A mixture of styles has the effect of making the reader pass through a succession of contradictory and ambiguous attitudes; it offers no sure stylistic norm by which the reader may orient him or herself permanently to the fiction and to the point of view of the author" (218–19). To put it slightly differently, not only the vocabularies but the values and visions they reflect are shown to be both tenable and arbitrary. The presentation of mixed-style projects—particularly those in which the mix occurs not only at the level of chapter (*As I Lay Dying,* for example) but also at the level of the sentence (*Mulligan Stew,* for example)—thereby becomes a mode of decenterment, demystification, detotalization, and delegitimation.

By employing discursive slapstick, Barthelme enters the company of a number of other postmodern comedians. Angela Carter's short stories, Sukenick's *Blown Away,* and Beckett's fiction come immediately to mind. And Pynchon also comes to mind, along with the verbal anarchy he performs in *Gravity's Rainbow,* an anarchy that leads to the downfall of his narrator(s)'s attempt at self-confident syntax, and thus, perhaps, his/their frequent breathless stutter.

While such linguistic ruptures in Pynchon's text often occur at the level of page-long passages such as in the long discussion of polymers (the lexical field of the chemist) or the derivation of a phrase like "Shit 'n' Shinola" (the lexical field of the etymologist), they also occur at the level of paragraph and sentence. Such prose, reminiscent of chameleonic Gavin Trefoil himself, manifests as well an extremely high information density, the result of a chaotic epic cataloguing of a grotesquely decadent universe. It is, as Rosemary Jackson points out, a prose that "gathers together a massive amount of cultural material as if it were so much waste matter, the waste of 'culture,' culture *as* waste, or garbage or excrement, on the page" (166). Like Borges's Funes, Pynchon's text could well claim that "my memory, sir, is like a garbage disposal" (*Ficciones* 112). Pynchon's frequent echoes of Norman O. Brown and all of his scatological references indicate what has gone terribly wrong with Western culture. Slothrop's journey down the toilet that I mentioned at the beginning of this study is not just an example of dark humor at work. It is also a vision of our culture as so much excrement, a vision of the underside of our civilization of excess, a vision of our culture's descent into what Walker Percy has dubbed the "Thanatos Syndrome."

The projects of these postmodern comedians refuse centrism, total intelligibility, closure and absolute "significance." They take nothing very seriously, including their own artistry and their own ability to make sense. Theirs is an impulse to go around "deconstructing dreams like nobody's business" (*Sixty Stories* 453). From this point of view they are the logical aesthetic extension of the philosophical trajectory that might, according to Beckett, find its launch site in Descartes and his follower Geulincx, certainly in Nietzsche, and rockets V-2–like through Wittgenstein, Heidegger, Saussure, and, in a parallel arc, Schrödinger, Heisenberg, and Bohr, to land at the feet of Derrida, who looks back at least as much to the tradition of the Keystone Kops as he does to that of Husserl or Freud.

Consequently, the postmodern comedians come to represent, on the one hand, the negative drive toward disruptions of human systems—of the Cartesian belief that all science might one day be unified through a rational method and that the universe will thereby become utterly interpretable, of humanist art and its moral emphasis on the dignity and central position of man in the universe. The postmodern comedians are suspicious of the so-called rational humanism, expressed to a greater degree in Davenport's project and less in Nabokov's and Burgess's, which has produced toxic waste, ICBMs, and a Pynchonesque Immachination that has brought our culture to the

113

edge of extinction. They are suspicious of our belief in the shared speech, shared values, and shared perceptions that we would like to believe form our culture but that are in fact fictions that exist, as the narrator of "Me and Miss Mandible" says, only as part of the "debris of our civilization" and the "vast junkyard" (*Sixty Stories* 25) of our planet.

At the same time, and equally if paradoxically as important, the postmodern comedians represent a positive or recuperative drive that as well has much to do with Nietzsche, Wittgenstein, and the rest. At the same time the postmodern comedians haphazardly undertake destruction of our basic assumptions about language and experience, they also create willy-nilly the possibility for construction of a new set of assumptions about language and experience that are more appropriate to our situations as we prepare to enter a new century. By their very negations, the postmodern comedians wittily, wonderfully, and touchingly affirm the power of the human imagination. They open up for a moment a colorful point of potential, suspension, and toleration for multiple views that might in the end lead us out of our current grave predicament and into a new frame of reference that might well be a new renaissance following on the heels of this second Middle Ages.

V
OUTSIDE THE BIGTOP

7.
Pragmatism, Politics, and Postmodernism, or: Leaving the White Hotel

> What is more to the point is the overall feeling of the white hotel, its wholehearted commitment to orality—sucking, biting, eating, gorging, taking in, with all the blissful narcissism of a baby at the breast. Here is the oceanic oneness of the child's first years, the auto-erotic paradise, the map of our first country of love.
> —Thomas, *The White Hotel*

Raising the Kids, Teaching the Students

An alternative, if less clearly defined, philosophical trajectory exists beside that of the postmodern comedian, and it is a deeply American one at that—although, according to its proponents, its flight path tracks back through the British tradition of Mill, Hume, and Locke to the launch site of Aristotle, Protagoras, and Socrates. It is a trajectory highly suspicious of intellectualist academic philosophy. It seeks meaning in praxis, in the concrete, in nitty-gritty facts. Less a generalized system of truth than a practical technique for finding solutions to philosophical problems and for promoting successful communication, it is in many ways the antimatter of postmodernism. Although it is often associated with Peirce and Dewey, it was made famous and embodied by William James during the last years of the nineteenth century and the first of the twentieth.

Jamesian pragmatism asks some strikingly levelheaded questions about ideas, or at least it appears to do so through the eyes of those nurtured on the Anglo-American tradition. "A pragmatist turns his back resolutely and once for all upon a lot of inveterate habits dear to professional philosophers," James writes, and there can be no more purified professional philosophers than the postmoderns, who have raised self-consciousness and theory to a paralytic level. The pragmatist "turns away from abstraction and insufficiency, from verbal solutions, from bad *a priori* reasons, from fixed principles, closed systems, and pretended absolutes and origins. He turns towards concreteness and adequacy, towards facts, towards action and towards power" (45). Pragmatism rhymes with nominalism, James continues, in its love of particulars. It rhymes with utilitarianism in its love of the practical. And it rhymes with positivism in its disdain for useless questions and metaphysical generalizations (47). Ideas are not just airy play toys to fool with freely but are things that become relatively true *"just in so far as they help us to get into satisfactory relations with other parts of our experience"* (49, James's italics), just in so far as they help us get along in our day-to-day world. Jamesian pragmatism deflates the pretension of metaphysics by asking what the plain plump consequences of an idea are: "What difference would it practically make to any one if this notion rather than that notion were true?" (42).

Hassan looks toward this brand of pragmatism for a possible solution to what he sees as the postmodern dilemma, and he has begun to suggest that pragmatism is making a comeback on the intellectual scene. He recounts, for example, how even the French in the person of Yves Bonnefoy, Barthes's successor at the Collège de France, argues in his inaugural address that we must again begin to emphasize presence over absence and human relations over language. Hassan locates the contemporary pragmatic moment in Richard Rorty's project, which underscores a commitment to *"beliefs in action rather than ironies of theories"* (Hassan's italics), and asserts that "pragmatism is intimate with all the uncertainties of our postmodern condition without quiescence, sterility, or abdication of judgment" (*Postmodern Turn* 205).

Certainly, a number of thinkers have begun asking postmodernism a number of painfully pragmatic questions. In *Small World: An Aca-*

demic Romance, for instance, David Lodge writes about a deconstructionist kidnapped by Italian terrorists—in other words, about a postmodern theoretician placed in a universe of praxis. Upon his release, the kidnapped academic comes to realize that he has lost his faith in deconstruction because "death is the one concept you can't deconstruct. Work back from there and you end up with the old idea of an autonomous self. I can die, therefore I am" (328). In *White Noise,* DeLillo's character Jack Gladney, a professor of Hitler Studies at a small liberal arts college, arrives at a similar conclusion. After a toxic cloud descends on his town and infects him with death, Jack comes to see that the academy is as much a part of the world, or the world as much a part of the academy, as anything else. Death is all around Jack, and in him as well. Theorizing about the likenesses between Elvis and Hitler is fun but useless. Nothing *really* matters in this culture of dreck. One can't *really* trust anyone. Speaking to Winnie, a research neurochemist who has been analyzing a pill Jack's wife has been taking to quell her fear of death, Jack asks:

> "What do I do to make death less strange? How do I go about it?"
> "I don't know."
> "Do I risk death by driving fast around curves? Am I supposed to go rock climbing on weekends?"
> "I don't know," she said. "I wish I knew."
> "Do I scale the sheer facade of a ninety-story building, wearing a clip-on belt? What do I do, Winnie? Do I sit in a cage full of African snakes like my son's best friend? This is what people do today."
> "I think what you do, Jack, is forget the medicine in this tablet. This is no medicine, obviously."
> She was right. They were all right. Go on with my life, raise my kids, teach my students. (229–30)

There is nothing like a good dose of death to bring one out of the realm of theory and verbal games, and to cement one firmly to the realm of fact, experience, and action. There is nothing like a good dose of death to force one to reexamine the important practical questions about life and understand at some very basic level that freeplay is never completely free, that there is an eternity between presence and absence. Robert Alter's words may serve as a parable for this. He discusses the difference between playing with language and playing with things, then adds: "We are free to decenter, deconstruct, decode, re-encode a tiger in a text, but even the hardiest structuralist would not step inside the cage with the real beast, whose fangs and claws, after all, are more than a semiotic pattern" (233).

Rereading Postmodernity

Even Pynchon, one of the postmodern apostles, questions the essence of postmodernism when, in that well-known passage about the comfort of paranoia and the destabilizing bliss of anti-paranoia, he adds that anti-paranoia is "a condition not many of us can bear for long" (*Gravity's Rainbow* 434).

The universe might be all the things the postmodern believes it is, but that doesn't mean he or she can endure it in its raw state. Practically speaking, at an ontological level, there is a limit to our tolerance as a species to the polymorphous perversity of postmodernism, to the delightful destabilization of its humor. Postmodernism, as Baudrillard says, is an analogue for schizophrenia. The question is: How many of us can actually stand to be schizophrenic for long? Postmodernism is an antisystem, but how many of us can actually reject *all* systems? Teaching, after all, is part of a system. Stopping at a red light is part of a system. Receiving a paycheck is part of a system. To live in absolute openness means not living for very long—and having a disorienting time of it, too. Perhaps one of the more charming ironies in all this is that those people who make it their living to think about antisystems and the flaws of the Western philosophical tradition have bought into—economically, politically, socially, and bureaucratically—an academic system that is of course a direct outgrowth of the Western philosophical tradition they seek to undermine. It appears they understand James's notion of cash value in a fundamental way.

Another perhaps less charming irony that occurs at a political level centers on the concept that postmodernity has democratized art, opened it to everyone, and hence has turned its back on the "cryptofascistic" elitism of modernity. While it is surely true, as Huyssen and others believe, that postmodern art is often the product of minds deluged by a mass culture of B-movies, comic books, television shows, superstars, popular events, and rock 'n' roll, it does *not* follow that such minds, when expressed in art, are necessarily democratic and accessible. The technique used to bring such eclectic scraps of the past together—the pastiche, the heteroglossia—tends to transform the postmodern artifact into a work at least as inaccessible and elite as *The Waste Land* or *Ulysses*. One need only think of *Gravity's Rainbow, Mulligan Stew,* or *Blown Away* to understand just how antidemocratic such art really is. It may be argued that postmodernity has simply replaced one sort of elitism with another.

At the same time that the postmodern claims to democratize, however, it also and paradoxically claims to destabilize. Another question arises here at the aesthetic level: How long can a text have the desired effect of destabilization? Walter Abish intuits this situation when he asks if a reader in the last few years of the twentieth century can still think of Robbe-Grillet as an experimental writer. Kathryn Hume understands it as well, when, in her study of Pynchon, she says that the nature of our reading changes each time we confront a given text. She argues that, surely, the first time we read a book like *Gravity's Rainbow* we are baffled by the text's gleeful decomposition of nineteenth-century novelistic norms. We feel "acute anxiety, a 'paranoid' desire to connect anything with anything that seems remotely connectable, frustration that no connections work really well, and considerable resentment" (199).

Just as surely, though, this *isn't* our reaction on subsequent readings. Rather, on our next trek through the book we are "likely to feel triumph at piecing fragments together into larger patterns, pleasure at remembering characters and places and at being now able to connect them to major plot lines" (200). Obviously, many of the maps we create for ourselves will be flawed by contradictions, but for the active reader coherent themes and images will emerge. By the third, fourth, and fifth readings, anxiety and the sense of destabilization have largely disappeared. Certainly, we cannot tie everything together, but we have learned not to worry about that. We understand that the text will never be fully comprehensible, but we no longer feel radically unsettled in our thought processes. The more one experiences a postmodern text, the less postmodern it becomes for the simple reason that humans need to make sense of their environments. They need to be able to create meaning in the texts around them, even if that meaning is in some way informed by the knowledge that the text cannot be *wholly* knowable. Give them an inkblot, and they will construct a coherent narrative. Give them a narrative, and they will construct a coherent interpretation.

Inherent contradictions consequently arise in the idea of the postmodern at the levels of ontology, politics, and aesthetics. Moreover, as I suggested at the outset of this book, to name some mode of consciousness *postmodernism* is to begin to construct a narrative and hence an interpretation. To do so is to begin to objectify and stabilize a way of thinking whose desire is to remain unnameable and destabilized. The instant critics began to comprehend that something new was on the horizon, the sun of postmodernism began to set. The moment the critics articulated the presence of absence, an antisystem began to turn into a merely negative system. To say that postmodernity explores the impossibility of imposing a single meaning on a text through both the minimalism of degree-zero writing (Kafka, Borges, and Handke) and the maximalism of plurisignification (Sorrentino, Pynchon, and Melville) is, of course, to impose a meaning on a text, to create a menu, and the rest is a move toward the past, toward literary history.

Remarginalizing Postmodernity

Any postmodern must ultimately turn his or her mode of detotalization on itself, point toward its own internal ironies, inconsistencies, flawed assumptions, doublelogics, and implicit hierarchies. Any comedian must ultimately become the brunt of his or her own joke, expose his or her face to the last pie. Postmodern humor thereby reaches its own limit, begins to twist in upon itself, begins to conclude.

The rise of neorealism since the middle of the 1970s is one register of this conservative impulse within our culture. Fiction by such writers as Thomas McGuane, Tobias Wolff, and Ann Beattie expresses a certain nostalgia for the pragmatism of the nineteenth and early twentieth centuries, for the aesthetics of a Flaubert and Hemingway, although I should be quick to point out that neorealism isn't simply a resurgence of the old realism, or, more correctly, the old realisms. Rather, it is a realism that has moved through the blast furnace of postmodernity and come out on the other side, never able to be quite the same again.

The practitioners of neorealism seem to sense that, as Larry McCaffery and Sinda Gregory argue, "the theoretical concerns of the previous generation—the impassioned skirmishes over such issues as realism versus experimentalism, moral versus 'immoral' fiction, self-reflexive versus mimetic forms—have lost their energy" (1). Its practitioners seem to accept that realism isn't by definition necessarily nonexperimental or nonsubversive, that realism isn't necessarily one thing. Hence, one finds the mythological realism of Max Apple in *The Oranging of America* next to the folk realism of Toni Morrison in *Tar Baby* next to the minimal mysterious realism of Raymond Carver in *Cathedral*. In each case, however, this is a pared-down realism generated by a consumer culture of detritus, a "dirty realism," as Bill Buford suggests in his special issue of *Granta,* "about the belly-side of contemporary life, but . . . [a] realism so stylized and particularized—so insistently informed by a discomforting and sometimes elusive irony—that it makes the more traditional realistic novels of, say, Updike or Styron seem ornate, even baroque in comparison" (4). In other words, such a realism in whatever form it takes is essentially ironic in nature, a narrative mode that concerns itself with what is below the surface, with the disjunction between what is said (or, in the case of such writers as Jayne Anne Phillips and Frederick Barthelme, what is *not* said) and what is meant. Such writing might well indicate "that the aesthetic disruptions of the '60s indeed opened up new options for fiction," as McCaffery and Gregory assert (3), but it also expresses a fundamentally conservative vision of reality—a vision that wishes to conserve a humanist optic through which one looks backwards rather than ahead.

I must quickly add here that, whereas in our dominant culture postmodernity has begun to be remarginalized, in many subcultures it never began. Wherever there existed pockets of people who believed in totalizing systems, in metanarratives, postmodernity failed to reach its flashpoint. One thinks of a region in the United States such as Appalachia, and of its metanarrative of the folk expressed in works like James Still's *Pattern of Man and Other Stories,* Wendell Berry's *Nathan Coulter,* and Gurney Norman's mythologically structured *Divine Right's Trip.* Postmodernity at its most dominant was an urban mode of consciousness. It was a mode of consciousness that never reached Lynchburg, Virginia—nor much of academia for that matter.

I neither mean to launch an attack against postmodernity nor to claim that it is dead. Rather, I simply mean to describe several (though certainly not all) potential problems that are perceived by the neoconservatives—be they realists, naturalists, or modernists—to beat arrhythmically at the heart of postmodernity, problems that postmodernity itself and critics of postmodernity have begun to sense, and problems that have marked a kind of boundary to the postmodern enterprise. I also mean to suggest that postmodernity is no longer the dominant mode of consciousness in our culture. In recent years it has been nudged aside by a more conservative narratological and metaphysical stance, though it certainly still manifests itself in numerous ways and in numerous loci. Perhaps I should even go so far as to assert that the most efficacious locus that the postmodern has found for itself is at the margins of our cultural consciousness, as that which works when our heads are momentarily turned, when our eyes are momentarily closed, that voice of dissonance and dissidence, of radical skepticism that continually and subtly challenges our fundamental cultural assumptions.

The White Hotel

Much of what I have just said will become clearer if we turn to D. M. Thomas's *The White Hotel* (1981), a book that embodies the pragmatic marginalization of the postmodern. The text begins as a humorous text that doesn't take much of anything seriously, but soon the solemn intrudes, the world turns dark, and an ironic tension erupts between a belief in the-universe-as-joke and a belief in the-universe-as-horror. Into the midst of frivolous self-reflexivity and intellectual gaming thunders the dread practical power of praxis.

Thomas chooses as his epigraph lines from Yeats's "The Stare's Nest by My Window," the sixth section of "Meditations in Time of Civil War." Speaking of the Irish freedom fighters' dark solution of fratricide and destruction, Yeats writes, "We had fed the heart on fantasies, / The heart's grown brutal from the fare." At this late point in the poem, the reader has moved through images of order and harmony, such as the ancestral houses and the tower itself, and has come to focus on images of chaos and senseless violence. The nineteenth-century fantasies of revolution and freedom have given way to twentieth-century visions of brutality and ruin. In the poem's last image, Yeats turns away from what the civil war has wrought, from what has been lost and from what is to come, and claims he finds as much solace as he needs in occult investigations, the "abstract joy" and "half-read wisdom" of "daemonic images." Put another way, he turns from one system (the political) toward another (the metaphysical).

At first, Thomas's epigraph seems to signal that ours is a time that has been fed so long on its *political* fantasies that it has become brutal from its fare. But Thomas's use of Yeats's lines also seems to indicate that being fed on *any* fantasies, any systems whatsoever, can contribute to violence. There is a suggestion here, then, that occult, aesthetic and psychoanalytic systems have had as much to do with our "senseless tumult" as have political ones. Perhaps Thomas has turned Yeats's quote against itself in an attempt to interrogate modern assumptions about the value of totalizing models and to ask what positive solutions such models have contributed to our culture. The result of this ambiguity is to transform the text that follows into a series of questions rather than possible answers.

The "Prologue," which begins on 8 September 1909, the year of Freud and Jung's famous trip to America, and concludes in Vienna on 18 May 1931, two years before Paul von Hindenburg appointed Hitler chancellor, frames the novel in an epistolary mode. Its narrative strategy announces the text as one concerned with multiple perspectives, relative truths, as one that strives against any kind of overview. The first letter, written by Sandor Ferenczi, introduces us to the man whom Thomas calls in his author's note the "discoverer of the great and beautiful modern myth of psychoanalysis." Freud is slightly pompous, slightly silly, and surely brilliant. In a luxurious Bremen hotel on the eve of their departure, Jung begins talking about his fascination with the peat-bog mummies either drowned or buried in the marshes of northern Germany (an image that prefigures those corpses first buried in Babi Yar then "drowned" when a dam is built across the mouth of the ravine and water is pumped in "creating a green, stagnant and putrid lake" [298]), and Freud first becomes agitated, then gruff, and finally he faints (5). The hint already appears that the creator of a myth to account for individual trauma cannot deal with historical trauma.

In the next letter, written just after World War I, Freud comments that he often visits the Vienna General Hospital to investigate the "allegations of ill-treatment of war neurotics" (8). What he emphasizes, however, is not the war, but the neuroses. He apparently cannot make the connection between the manifestation of individual neuroses and the manifestation of the communal. The third letter makes the first reference to Elizabeth Erdman, "a young woman of most respectable character" (10), "normally shy and prudish" (11), who has produced "a somewhat extraordinary 'journal' " (10). Freud, who continually makes gestures toward scientific objectivity, nevertheless couches his comments in the language of the subjective moralist. We repeatedly find, then, a myopic character with at least a contradictory nature, at most a hypocritical one, certainly one in any case that the reader must treat as potentially unreliable.

"Don Giovanni" radically and abruptly disrupts narrative modes by switching from the epistolary to the poetic. Faulkner might have claimed with respect to a modern text such as *Absalom, Absalom!* that "the truth . . . comes out, that when the reader has read all these thirteen different ways of looking at the blackbird, the reader has his own fourteenth image of that blackbird which I would like to think is the truth" (Gwynn and Blotner 273–74), but here we realize there will be no fourteenth image, no ultimate truth. *The White Hotel*'s heteroglossia is designed to subvert such notions. This first chapter, which Thomas published as an individual poem in the magazine *New Worlds* in 1979, is Elizabeth Erdman's highly erotic account of her imagined sexual adventure with Freud's son. As Hana Wirth-Nesher comments, it is also an expression of double-transference from patient to physician to physician's son. It is the product of an oceanic consciousness that refuses the male notion of boundaries. It is written between the staves of the score of Mozart's 1787 opera, which is based on the legend of Don Juan whose conquests include well over two thousand women.

Elizabeth both overturns the stereotype of male as aggressor by assuming Don Giovanni's position as libertine and at the same time, paradoxically, reveals her Victorian moralism by identifying with a rake who is punished for his sexual abandon by suffering an eternity in hell. Just as in Mozart's opera the erotic is associated with the violent, so too here eros is associated with thanatos:

then he rammed in again you can't conceive
how pure the stars are, large as maple leaves
up in the mountains, they kept falling falling
into the lake, we heard some people calling,
we think the falling stars were Leonids,
and for a time one of his fingers slid
beside his prick in me there was so much room,
set up a crosswise flutter, in the gloom
bodies were being brought to shore, we heard
a sound of weeping, his finger hurt (19)

Drowning (another prefiguration of Babi Yar) is linked to frantic sex. Romantic images of stars, flowers, and the lake, all suggesting an ideal state of peace and tranquility, are linked to morbid images of people calling for help, people crying, and bodies being brought to shore, all suggesting a prosaic state of suffering and death. Pornography, pain, doom, and beautiful poetry are fused and confused, seeming to prove Freud's earlier assertion that "I am on the right lines in positing a death instinct, as powerful in its own way (though more hidden) as the libido" (9). The life instinct, which is concerned with self-preservation and preservation of the species as well as with establishing unities, operates against and combines with the death instinct, which is concerned with returning to an earlier inorganic state as well as with undoing connections (see chapter 2 in *An Outline of Psycho-Analysis*). Soon another expression of the life instinct located in the romantic tradition, German Nazism, will lead to a number of huge and horrible manifestations of the reifying death instinct.

"The Gastein Journal," which Elizabeth creates when Freud asks her "to go away and write down her own analysis of the material she ha[s] produced, in a restrained and sober manner" (133), is an expanded prose version of the "Don Giovanni" composition "unti-

126

d[ily]" (133) written in a child's exercise book. Although Freud feels Elizabeth took his suggestion "not unreasonably as a rebuke" (133) against her composition of "Don Giovanni," there is also the possibility that Freud has again misread the situation. Through a different optic, the Gastein journal is a rebuke of Freud. After all, rather than delivering up "an interpretation, as [Freud] had asked, [Elizabeth] ha[s] chosen to expand her original phantasy, embroidering every other word, so that [Freud] seem[s] to have gained nothing except the herculean task of reading a document of great length and untidiness" (133). Elizabeth simply transforms her poem into prose, and, by doing so, she tweaks Freud's puritan nose by giving him "an erogenous flood, an *inundation* [we are back, it should be noted, to the image of the flood] of the irrational and libidinous" (133). She exerts her subjectivity upon his need for objectivity. She exerts her will. Her creation of the heteroglossia of postcards from different hotel guests on roughly the same topics, as Mary F. Robertson has pointed out, "depicts synecdochally [the] arbitrariness in written signs" (461). Such a gesture is analogous to Derrida's notion that writing is cut off from both author and authority. It attacks ideas of the scientific and the center, the very ideas that Freud embodies.

Here we also begin to learn more about Elizabeth's gift for prophecy. It is not for nothing that Thomas has chosen this name for his protagonist. For the Franciscans, Elizabeth of Hungary, who is especially venerated in Germany, stands for charity, wears a triple crown symbolic of her three states (virgin, wife, and widow), and is often depicted tending the sick. Another Elizabeth, the mother of Saint John the Baptist, is often shown at the Massacre of the Innocents, fleeing the carnage, her child John the Baptist hidden in her cloak. Freud also gives his patient the name Anna G(iovanni?), one which recalls Donna Anna from Mozart's opera, the prophetess described by Saint Luke (2:36), and Freud's own youngest child. These echoes complement each other and sound throughout the text. The Gastein journal begins with a prophetic image of a massacre of innocents that looks forward to the one that will take place in the fifth chapter: Elizabeth's nightmare attempt to escape pursuing soldiers and to help a bleeding boy on the way. Later, we find that often during intercourse with her anti-Semitic husband Elizabeth hallucinates about falling from great heights and about mourners being buried in a landslide (144), just as she will fall from a great height into the ravine at Babi Yar and be covered with earth and water. The pain in her left breast and ovary and her shortness of breath apparently are not the psychosomatic symptoms of sexual repression, as Freud would have

127

it, but premonitions of the SS man kicking her in the left breast at the bottom of the ravine at Babi Yar (293), her bayonet rape (294), and her drowning (296). She becomes a modern Cassandra whose predictions no one believes. She is the daughter of a Jewish father (though Freud delegates such information to a footnote [145]), and she becomes the emblem of Victim in the twentieth century, woman and Jew.

"Frau Anna G," the third chapter, takes the form of a case study by Freud of Elizabeth, similar in logic and style to his well-known study of Dora. It thereby marks another radical narrative shift. So far Elizabeth has told her own story in the body of the text via poem and prose. Now Freud attempts to make her part of *his* story. By transforming Elizabeth into a third-person character in his clinical account, Freud in his first-person narrative fashions her into an object of secondary importance. From the beginning, Freud tries to mold Elizabeth Erdman into something other than Elizabeth Erdman. He even changes her name and tries to alter her identity for the purposes of his science. To put it another way, he centers her as an object of study. He defines her selfhood. He seeks control over her. By doing so, he finally makes her into another kind of victim—science's.

Freud constructs a labyrinthine interpretation of Elizabeth's symptoms. As a believer in a metaphysics of presence, he searches for the stable meaning behind her "hysteria," primarily through dream analysis. What he finds, not surprisingly, considering that he is working within a closed self-validating system, is that her problems originated in childhood and among the dynamics of the family. In essence, Freud decides that Elizabeth's symptoms—pain in her left breast and ovary and shortness of breath—which Elizabeth is convinced are organic in nature, are in fact the result of a repressed memory of an apparent sexual tryst between her mother and uncle in the family's summerhouse. The memory, Freud writes, "was too disturbing and puzzling, and the child forgot it in play. The adult Anna, when it flashed back to her with all the accretions of mature knowledge, immediately assumed the worst; and likewise found it impossible to bear" (156). In addition, Elizabeth was never close to her cold Jewish father and hence could not be close to other men. Her idealized Catholic mother died with her brother-in-law in a fire in Moscow and, as a result, Elizabeth felt guilty about her mother's death, the Oedipal matricide literally enacted, and sought the love of surrogate mothers such as Madame Kedrova in an act of latent homosexuality. Indeed, her final longing is for the wonderful womb of the white hotel, an analogue for her mother's body, a blissful narcissistic "haven of security" (166) where all is unified and "there is no division between Anna and the world outside" (135).

Throughout the course of their sessions, Elizabeth remains unconvinced that her symptoms are merely psychosomatic, and she argues strongly against Freud's assertion that she is an unacknowledged lesbian. Freud, of course, testily counters that she must be repressing. He claims that the pains in her left breast and ovary are manifestations of "her unconscious hatred of her distorted feminity" and that her shortness of breath is "a consequence of having glimpsed the true circumstances of her mother's death." To the end, however, he is unsure why the pain afflicts the left side of her body, though he guesses that "it may be that there was a propensity to illness in the patient's left breast and ovary." He concludes that "no analysis is ever complete; the hysterias have more roots than a tree," but that in any case Elizabeth "felt practically restored to health" and "was anxious to take up her musical career" (164). With that they part "on friendly terms" (165).

"The Health Resort," the fourth chapter, is the story of Elizabeth's life beyond therapy from 1929 to 1936 and it is told in an appropriately stable narrative mode, mimetic realism à la nineteenth-century novels. Elizabeth gains gradual success as an opera singer. She marries a widowed Russian Jew, the husband of her idol who died in childbirth. She adopts his son, Kolya. More interesting, however, is that she also begins to decompose Freud's beautiful modern myth. Freud himself was inadvertently already well along the way to doing so in "Frau Anna G." He makes claims of nonjudgmentalism, but in fact abridges, edits, synthesizes, and subjectively interprets ambiguous situations and continually judges Elizabeth harshly when she is either evasive or does not accept his interpretations. In many ways and contrary to his own opinion, Freud is more artist than scientist. He creates stories that have little to do with communal reality but much to do with the production of an aesthetic pattern that makes sense of otherwise nonsensical data.

This is further substantiated when, in the series of letters she exchanges with Freud in 1931, Elizabeth confesses that reading his case history "has been like reading the life story of a young sister who is dead—in whom I can see a family resemblance yet also great differences: characteristics and actions that could never have applied to me." She adds that "you saw what I allowed you to see" and that "it was not your fault that I seemed to be incapable of telling the truth" (214). Elizabeth has changed from a weak hysteric to a successful and independent woman.

129

Freud may have been Elizabeth's muse, but, as Robertson writes, there is a possibility that she progresses "in spite of Freud rather than because of him" (457). Freud and Elizabeth have vied for power throughout. Freud seeks control over Elizabeth, and Elizabeth seeks control over her own life. She does what she has to to survive, and part of what she does entails telling Freud a series of "lies and half-truths" (*The White Hotel* 216). It turns out that she wrote her "Don Giovanni" long before Freud asked her to. She fails to tell him that, when she was three, she came across her mother, aunt, and uncle engaged in "intercourse *a tergo*" (216) on her father's yacht. She lies about her first lover's brutality to her on the yacht in the Gulf of Finland, claiming "it was a beautiful weekend . . . and for me at least it was wonderful" (219). Perhaps most important, she lies about being accosted by the sailors on the merchant ship, who allegedly abused her because of her mother's loose reputation. The truth is that they abused her sexually because she was Jewish, but she keeps this information from Freud because, as she says, "I knew you were Jewish . . . and it seemed shameful to be ashamed" (221). Moreover, even though her father was kind to her after this event, she still blamed him for it because he was Jewish. Even more strange to Elizabeth is that she found her abuse arousing; in fact, she masturbates while remembering what the sailors did to her (222). She also withholds from Freud a lesbian encounter with Elizabeth's father's chambermaid because she worries that Freud will find justification of his theory of latent homosexuality. "But isn't adolescence a time of experimentation?" she writes to him. "It was all very innocent, and never happened again, with her or anyone" (222). She concludes that she, like Freud, cannot explain her pains, though they still continue to haunt her, and she suggests to him that after reading about all of her deceptions "you may feel that your case study needs changing— or even abandoning" (216).

Surely, an objective observer would have to agree with Elizabeth. But Freud replies that "I prefer to go ahead with the case study as it stands, despite all imperfections." He is "willing," however, "to add a postscript in which your later reservations are presented and discussed," though he also adds one last reprimand: "I shall feel compelled to make the point that the physician has to trust his patient, quite as much as the patient must trust the physician" (230). Freud transforms Elizabeth's lies into "reservations" and hints that it is her fault that he must tag on an addendum. In her next letter to Freud, she confesses remorse that her premonition of Freud's grandson's death might have caused the death, but Freud quickly passes over this reply, saying "my experience of psychoanalysis has convinced me that telepathy exists" (231). At some level he acknowledges Elizabeth's gift of second sight, but he still struggles with her for dominance in the psychological universe he inhabits—the very universe that can do nothing to account for what happens in the last two chapters of the text.

Freud cannot deal with Elizabeth's Jewishness. Concerned as he is with the depth of the individual, he cannot see or understand the realm of the communal. Committed as he is to the realm of the psychological, he cannot see or understand the realm of the political. This is borne out in "The Sleeping Carriage," chapter five, the account of Elizabeth's and Kolya's last day on Earth, which culminates in their terrible deaths, along with those of thirty-three thousand others, at Babi Yar on 29 and 30 September 1941. As Lady Falls Brown has demonstrated and as Thomas himself states on his acknowledgments page, much of this section closely parallels Anatoli Kuznetsov's documentary novel, *Babi Yar,* particularly the section concerning Dina Pronicheva's testimony.

In "The Sleeping Carriage" we come to fully understand the ramifications of Freud's myopia, and that his psychoanalytic system is powerless before the horrifically forceful one of Nazism. Or, perhaps more to the point, we come to realize that the battle between the death instinct and the life instinct in our century has been raised to a cultural level. As Thomas comments in the *Times Literary Supplement,* "my heroine, Lisa Erdman, changes from being Lisa an individual to Lisa in history" (quoted by Wirth-Nesher 24). Freud is a late outrider of the Western culture, believing that self-discovery is possible through the careful exercise of reason. He becomes an analogue for the Cartesian and Newtonian universes. But we learn in the fifth chapter that neither the universe nor the self can be finally understood, that "the soul of man is a far country, which cannot be approached or explored" (*White Hotel* 294), and that "if a Sigmund Freud had been listening and taking notes from the time of Adam, he would still not fully have explored even a single group, even a single person" (295). Freudian analysis is impotent in the face of utter political menace. The pragmatic is injected at this point by the implicit question raised: What good is Freudianism in the face of social responsibility?

What is important to Elizabeth is not the psychoanalytic reading of her symptoms, but the ethical one. She reads her symptoms as organic rather than psychosomatic. "What torments me is whether life is good or evil" (226), she writes to Freud ten years before Babi Yar. In a world where, as Thomas writes, "imagination . . . is exhausted in the effort to take in the unimaginable which happened" (quoted by Wirth-Nesher 24), where "things are things so far beyond belief that it ought to be possible to awake from them" (*White Hotel* 288), Elizabeth chooses the moral over the psychological, the communal over the individual, the diachronic over the synchronic. Although she could have saved herself at Babi Yar since she had an out-of-date identity card saying her name was Erdman and her nationality Ukrainian, Elizabeth chooses to die with her stepson Kolya, whose legal name is Berenstein. The soldier at the entrance tells her "You're not a Yid, you don't have to go through old lady," but Elizabeth answers "But I *must!* . . . I *am* a Yid! . . . I *am!* My father was a Yid. Please believe me" (282). Instead of choosing the personal identity Freud wanted her to choose, she chooses the social identity that will mean her death. Paradoxically, however, at the same moment in the narrative that she decides on the communal, she also becomes an individual. At the same moment she becomes an individual, she is turned into an object by the narrator's third-person point of view.

If the text concluded here, Thomas's purpose would have been relatively clear. The novel would have traced an arc from a narcissistic autoerotic physical perspective in chapters one and two, through the psychological in chapter three and a growing sense of self in relationship to the community in chapter four, to a strong moral sense of history in the fifth chapter. Following the implicit argument set up by this arc, then, we could see the novel as a progression of perceptions, an evolution of a person from self-centered to a fully mature and realized self. But Thomas gives us no such solution. Rather, he gives us an astonishingly incongruous sixth chapter, "The Camp," an obviously fantastic and edenic landscape in which Elizabeth ends up after a train journey (and here we should recall Freud's earlier remark that "train journeys are themselves dreams of death" [120]) and in which, in a kind of postwar Palestine, Elizabeth is reunited with her mother, Freud, and others.

If we keep in mind Freud's remark about train journeys, it is possible that this is a dream Elizabeth has as she is dying in the pit at Babi Yar. If we follow this hypothesis, Elizabeth's situation would become analogous to Peyton Farquhar's in Ambrose Bierce's "An Occurrence at Owl Creek Bridge," in which the bulk of the story, unbeknownst to the reader until the end, is comprised of Farquhar's dream of escape at the moment he is hanged. But such a reading falls back on a psychological approach, an approach that has been undermined by the course of the narrative itself.

The historical doesn't seem to help us either. While it is true that the landscape in the fifth chapter bears suspicious resemblance to Palestine after World War II, it clearly isn't a mimetic one because it is populated by the dead. Perhaps we should see this section, as Wirth-Nesher suggests, as yet another new mode of perception, this time theological, "Dante's Christian soul redeemed through faith and love" (26–27). But such a reading too is flawed since this is clearly no Christian heaven of redemption. After all, Elizabeth still limps, Freud still has a cancerous jaw, and the British soldier still has only one arm. There might be a virgin birth, but it is by a cat, not the mother of Jesus. Elizabeth, in a beautifully Christian moment, might comprehend that "wherever there is love, of *any* kind, there is hope of salvation," but this thought is followed by "an image of a bayonet flashing over spread thighs" (318). The scent of the pines might, in the final sentence of the text, make her "happy," but it also "trouble[s] her in some mysterious way" (322). She might tell Richard Lyons on the penultimate page that "we were made to be happy and to enjoy life," but Richard counters her assertion with a question: "*Were* we made to be happy?" (321).

Leaving the White Hotel

Just as Richard leaves Elizabeth with a question mark, so too the text leaves the reader with a series of interrogatives. The heaven of the last chapter is at best a kind of heavenly parody, another joke played upon the unsuspecting reader searching for the compensation of a Happy Ending. Behind the beatific images of Elizabeth sucking at her mother's breast, and her mother sucking at Elizabeth's, lies a series of practical questions: What happens when the Gestapo arrive? What place in this Palestine is there for Babi Yar? Does any kind of love really include the flash of a bayonet over spread thighs? Where is the Arab opposition and the wars of independence in this Israel?

As modern ironic readers, we long for stories, as did Freud, that produce aesthetic patterns that make sense of otherwise nonsensical data. But each story that Thomas has given us has been subverted by the one that has gone before and the one that comes after it. Each radical modal shift has reinforced the humorous postmodern notion that truth is unattainable, that there is no modern Faulknerian fourteenth blackbird.

At the same time, though, Thomas has also begun interrogating

133

the very postmodern premises he may have seemed at first to advo-
cate. His text indicates that ideas are things that become relatively
true *"just in so far as they help us to get into satisfactory relations
with other parts of our experience"* (49, James's italics), just in so far
as they help us get along in our day-to-day world. Each perspective
Thomas gives us in *The White Hotel*—be it physical, psychological,
political, or theological—is a coherent and viable language game or
micronarrative that gives meaning to our lives and helps us get
along. Each is arbitrary and incomplete, and yet useful. Simultaneously, his tentative and painfully self-aware text suggests that one
cannot live forever in the apolitical white hotel of postmodernity,
that "auto-erotic paradise" dedicated as it is to "all the blissful narcis-
sism of a baby at the breast" (134–35). The pragmatic Thomas
points to the bliss of pla(y)giarism, aesthetic sport, the boundless
mindcircus of "Don Giovanni," while he concurrently raises immensely important ethical questions that fly in the face of such
surface-oriented concerns.

At the very moment Thomas's text announces itself as a highly self-
reflexive, antimimetic, self-consuming postmodern artifact obsessed
with the history of narration, it also announces itself as a highly cen-
tered piece of modern mimetic holocaust fiction obsessed with the
history of a people, the history of Western civilization, the practical
morality of praxis, and the final connection between personal and
collective tragedy. We are back to a Janus-text that looks both ahead
and behind at once. We are back to the visions of Nabokov and Burgess, who are simultaneously systems-haters and questers for workable
systems. We are back to our image of the modern-postmodern continuum where our needle has begun to move away again from its limit
position at the postmodern and humorous extreme. We have entered a
certain ironic hesitancy, a certain stutter, a certain modern dissatisfac-
tion with the premises of the postmodern, which Walter Abish will
explore yet more fully, if unintentionally.

8.
Nostalgia and the Omega

Is it possible for anyone in Germany,
nowadays, to raise his right hand, for
whatever reason, and not be flooded by the
memory of a dream to end all dreams?
—Abish, *How German Is It*

Postmortemism

Postmodern orthodoxy claims that a discontinuous composition is somehow preferable to a continuous one because the former more clearly registers contemporary experience, deconstructs totalizing systems, and forces the reader into an active engagement with the text. Certainly Walter Abish believes this assertion in his early works. Abish, who first began writing fiction in 1970, constructed his first novel, *Alphabetical Africa* (1974), out of fifty-two chapters, the first twenty-six labelled A to Z, the second Z to A. In chapter "A," all words begin with the letter A, in chapter "B" A and B, and so forth. In the twenty-seventh chapter, things begin to work in reverse, words beginning with all the letters of the alphabet. In the twenty-eighth chapter all but Z is used to begin words, and so on, down to the last chapter, where again only A is used. As with Beckett's dramaticule *Breath*, there is a minimal movement of expansion and inevitable contraction. In his second collection of short stories, *In the Future Perfect* (1977), there appears a piece called "Ardor / Awe / Atrocity" where block paragraphs titled alphabetically with the basic vocabulary of the fiction appear, and each minifiction that follows employs a variation of the basic vocabulary given.

The purpose of such gestures is, according to Abish, to question "how we see and write about something" (Lotringer, "Interview" 2). For him, "the ideal text is one that cries for interpretation" (7), "language is at best unreliable" (5), characters have no "reality . . . outside the text" (3), and "to embrace the 'real' events [in a text] is to remain innocent. It is to embrace answers. That is, essentially, what the institutions in Western society churn out. A great many answers that authenticate the 'real' and 'familiar' world" (2). As an outcome, Abish's texts have been attacked by the "literary establishment" for being "literary game[s]" (Falkenberg), "subversive" (Malin) and "seemingly avant-garde work that fools judges and wins awards" (Baillet). (*How German Is It* "fooled" judges and won the PEN/ Faulkner Award for the most distinguished work of American fiction in 1980). At the same time, "literary experimentalists"—and here one must begin to wonder what kind of literature is *not* ultimately experimental—have lauded Abish for being "one of the most legitimately expressive writers of our time" (Klinkowitz) behind whose "*tour[s] de force*" (Knowlton) pulses "a vast emotional hinterland" (West).

But, to raise yet a further set of pragmatic problems with our subject, while postmodern orthodoxy might apply to a limited number of fictions, including Abish's early ones, it finally is reductionistic and inaccurate. It is incorrect to assume the traditional novel's satisfaction with plot reflects its satisfaction with society. If we can in fact generalize about works of writers as diverse as Stendhal and Henry James—and I am not at all sure that we can in any but the most superficial ways—we most definitely cannot draw the conclusion that a book has emotions, that a text can be either "satisfied" or "dissatisfied," as the postmodern claim intimates; such an assertion is a strange and misleading use of metaphor. Only the author who wrote the work or the reader who reads it can be satisfied or dissatisfied. And many traditional novelists and readers were anything *but* satisfied with society. Flaubert's *Madame Bovary* and Dostoevsky's *Notes from Underground,* to cite only two examples, have always been intended and read as indictments of bourgeois mentality.

Moreover, texts that are *not* postmodern can just as easily be structurally deformed or fragmented as postmodern texts while still containing moral centers or metanarratives. After all, Twain's *Huck Finn* has long been faulted for its flawed final chapters, and yet its stance against racism is clear and its archetypal pattern of departure, initiation, and reintegration with society has been common knowledge for nearly one hundred years. The myth of the Fisher King generates a coherent narrative beneath what only *seems* a text of mutilation in Eliot's *The Waste Land*. Ironically, then, postmodern orthodoxy attempts in spite of its criticophilosophical declarations to reduce multiplicity to a binary, and, as most of us intuit at some level, such a vision is myopic at best.

Whereas a career such as John Barth's has tended to move from the communal (*End of the Road*) to the authorial (*Lost in the Funhouse*), the tendency of Abish's has been to move from the authorial (*Alphabetical Africa*) to the communal (*How German Is It*). That is not to argue that *How German Is It* (1980) is simply a version of that mysterious "nineteenth-century novel" that, according to Robbe-Grillet, forms "the basis for tiresome parodies" (*For A New Novel* 135). (I should note here, though, that I have noticed a recent propensity to turn the *postmodern* novel into the basis for parody: a recent *Atlantic Monthly* ran a "review" of Derrida's "latest study," a deconstruction of *Winnie the Pooh*.) Rather, in *How German Is It*, as in *The White Hotel* and other texts as diverse as O'Brien's *Going After Cacciato*, Irving's *The World According to Garp*, Gaddis's *Carpenter's Gothic*, and Coetzee's *Foe*, at least two governing visions struggle for power in a complex way. At the stratum of structure, on the one hand, *How German Is It* is a thoroughly postmodern text. At the stratum of theme and character, however, it is a thoroughly modern— perhaps even premodern—one. *How German Is It* concurrently expresses a disenchantment with the postmodern and a longing for the center that Abish's earlier projects have tried to deconstruct. Such a disenchantment and textual ambivalence is typical of a large number of literary and theoretical works that are now somewhat carelessly and simplistically labelled "postmodern."

The English Garden Effect

How German Is It, according to Abish, grew out of "The English Garden," a short fiction in *In the Future Perfect* concerning an American who travels to Germany to interview a German writer. At the airport the American buys a coloring book and, during his brief stay, he continually compares the signs in the coloring book to other signs he finds in Germany. "That immediately reduces the landscape,"

Abish says, "to a set of signs and images and also introduces, not the interpretation itself, but the need for interpretation as well as the level on which the interpretation as well as the speculation is to be conducted" (Lotringer 4). The title of the short fiction recalls the English Garden Effect described by John Ashbery in Abish's epigraph—the idea that signs are self-reflexive, referring to the world only obliquely "to give the required air of naturalness, pathos and hope" (*In the Future Perfect* 1).

How German Is It holds within itself, as do *Lolita* and *The White Hotel*, a number of different kinds of texts: several varieties of the mimetic novel, fantasy, and metafiction. Each sends a different code to the reader concerning how it should be read. In addition, Abish's novel defamiliarizes the reading process through its splintered format and self-consumptive language. The result is a sense of dislocation on the reader's part, which marks the fulfillment of the text's deconstructive design. A traditional monologic narrative is replaced and subverted by a polyphonic one that refuses a stable and unified vision of experience, and the totalizing system of the traditional novel is thereby perverted and deformed. The text has been carnivalized, made humorous. Thus, *How German Is It* manifests what appears to be its essentially postmodern character.

Abish's novel initially seems to ask to be read as a mimetic text. It is a documentary about the New Germany as well as Ulrich Hargenau's pointless serial lovelife. It is as well an historical fiction about Ulrich's father, who, Ulrich claims, was executed by a firing squad one morning early in August 1944 for being one of the Stauffenberg Group, which tried to assassinate Hitler by setting off plastic explosives concealed in General Staff Colonel Claus Schenk Graf von Stauffenberg's briefcase during a conference at Wolfschanze, the führer's headquarters near Rastenburg in East Prussia.

But traces of the fantastic irrupt at the margins of the text. There is, of course, no way of knowing if von Hargenau was indeed executed, since there were as many as six hundred arrests connected with the incident (Hoffmann 512) and about two hundred executions (Hoffmann 528), but no mention of an Ulrich von Hargenau appears in the literature on the subject. More important, in his "son's" report there is apparently a factual slip that disarms the truth of the story. After the immediate reprisals by firing squad following the assassination attempt on 20 July, no one was executed again until *late* August, and then by *hanging*, not firing squad. In other words, Abish flags the possible fictionality and artificiality of his text and thereby underscores the irreality of his narrative and characters.

He further emphasizes this trace of the fantastic by introducing grotesque incidents and Kafkaesque agents into the novel. The mayor's wife's father, for example, has a heart attack while painting the mayor's house. He falls off the ladder on which he is balancing and dies—just a few feet below the room in which the mayor and his wife are passionately making love. Franz Metz, a servant in Helmut and Ulrich's house when they are children, spends much of his time researching and building a matchstick model of the Durst concentration camp. When he becomes agitated, he spends nights howling up in his room. Only his wife is "aware that his howls were in fact not uniform. Only she could immediately classify [each] howl and determine its cause" (73). Such gruesomely humorous thrusts in the text have so far been overlooked by critics, though Abish told me he considers his novel comic and though he has written that critics "cannot see the element of play in the book" because "the 'history' is too close" (Lotringer 2).

Another set of codes at play in the text are those from metafiction. The description the narrator gives of Ulrich's novel could serve as well as a description of Abish's book: "The characters in [Ulrich's] book can be said to be free of emotional disturbances, free of emotional impairments. They meet here and there . . . and without too much time spent analyzing their own needs, allow their brains a brief respite, as they embrace each other in bed" (16). Ulrich buys a secondhand copy of Victor Segalen's *Rene Leys* and finds that "in certain respects [it] paralleled or, at any rate, appeared analogous to his own endeavor in Geneva" (48). *Unser Deutschland,* the coloring book Daphne sends Ulrich, reminiscent of the one in Abish's "The English Garden," becomes a register of *How German Is It*'s intertextuality. On one page of the coloring book is a picture of "a schoolteacher, a young woman, in front of a blackboard" (177) who strikes the same pose as Anna Heller (119), the schoolteacher in Bromholdstein who purportedly encountered Paula in Ohlendorff and with whom Ulrich has a brief affair. The picture of "a work crew . . . repairing a sewer pipe in a long freshly dug trench" (117) rhymes with the ruptured sewer pipe in Brumholdstein that leads to the discovery of the mass grave (139). A third picture shows "a young man wearing a visored military cap and striped jersey astride a horse that was standing in a shallow part of a lake. The rider was barefoot and riding the horse bareback" (178)—a description of the cover of *How German Is It.*

Other Brechtian defamiliarizations evince themselves in the text at the level of format and language. The format of the novel takes the shape of splinters and spacing that indicate continual omissions, so the reader is made to feel s/he must guess at what is *not* there and must supplement various gaps. Speaking of the title of the text, which Abish is careful to point out lacks a question mark, he comments:

> The title calls attention to a preoccupation, in this case, Germany. It's a highly charged issue. Most of us have set responses to Germany, as we do to so much else. In general, readers compliantly accept what they are offered. Their chief concern is, "how readable is the text?" For the most part, novels about Germany, or those simply located in Germany, without having to raise the question of "How German is it" resolve the unspoken question by explaining Germany. In one way or another, they explain Germany away and thereby provide satisfaction. I have avoided an explanation. (Lotringer 1)

Question marks imply questions for which solutions can be found, but Abish on the contrary "sets up questions like a trap" (5) because he feels that "in life we are forever . . . confronted by situations that defy explanations. We simply do not have sufficient information about them" (4). Here one should remember that the essence of the postmodern is mutilation—a sign of impossibility, jammed expectations, and narrative incongruity.

Italicized questions and demands, the weak attainment of narrative motion by beginning paragraphs with the word *next* or *afterward,* abrupt switches in point of view (the sudden introduction, for instance, of Franz's, Anna's, or Gisela and Egon's sections), strange redundancy of phrasing (for example, "she found the exploration or probing of the relationship" [*How German Is It* 36]), and even the insertion of incorrect diction (substituting *persisting* for *insisting* in the sentence "The brain keeps persisting that it can survive on images alone" [17]) further contribute to the undermining of the reading process, the creation of "puzzles and mysteries" (Lotringer 4), the need for "what is left unsaid to remain a strong presence. As strong a presence as what is stated specifically" (6). Moreover, Abish's language is deliberately flat, often mechanical and minimal, suggestive of that by Handke, Bischel, and Kempowski, of whom the narrator of *How German Is It* makes mention (29). Impersonal expletives, state-of-being verbs, passive constructions, word redundancy, excessive subject-verb-predicate structures, and short declarative sentences all point to a language of self-consumption, the announcement of the void in a form without complexity, vitality, or individuality.

Such radical deformation of traditional structure seems to imply— if, again, we follow postmodern orthodoxy—the negative drive toward disruptions of human systems, of Cartesian reason, of humanist art and all it exemplifies. We have apparently reached Barthian exhaustion and Barthesian degree zero, where the reader finds only "a style of absence which is almost an ideal absence of style," where "writing is . . . reduced to a sort of negative mood" (*Writing Degree Zero* 77), where humanity has been deactivated, and where the dehuman and postcultural have surfaced.

Stepping in with the Tiger

If we move from how the work is put together (the various techniques) to the subject of the work (the ideas, characters, and so on presented via those various techniques), from the exterior to the interior of *How German Is It*, we discover, as we have in a number of the texts so far discussed, an early accessible chronology that indicates a belief in cause and effect. We discover fully rounded characters that suggest a belief in selfhood and psychology. We discover an allegiance to communal reality and a series of very human concerns: a pervasive sense of existential and political menace and paranoia, a link between individual and national trauma, and a certain nostalgia for a past that never existed. At the core of Abish's apparently polyphonic design beats a traditional monologic center that signals a stable and unified vision of experience the polyphonic design seems bent on dismantling.

How German Is It focuses on Ulrich Hargenau's life in a landscape pulsing with menace. One day a few weeks after Ulrich, a onetime radical and a writer working on a novel about his six-month love affair in Paris with a woman named Marie-Jean Filebra, returns from a year abroad, a yellow Porsche almost hits him. He cannot make out the driver, nor has he ever seen the car before. A passerby, we learn, "took it for granted that what he had just witnessed was an accident, just as Ulrich took it for granted that it was not" (11). Later, in Geneva, where Ulrich pursues his wife, Paula, he steps from a bookstore and catches a glimpse of Daphne Hasendruck, the terrorist who lied to Ulrich (telling him she is an American who came to Germany to study with Brumhold), and who has a short-term love affair with the writer in the passenger seat of a bright yellow Porsche. He receives threatening notes from the left-wing terrorist Einzieh Group, to which his wife belonged and against which he testified. While out walking one day in the woods with his brother, Helmut, Ulrich is shot in the arm by a man some distance away who slowly takes aim at him through the sights on his rifle. Several days later Ulrich finds out that the assassin is one of his brother's new friends. Everyone in Ulrich's universe is potentially dangerous. A threat always lies around the next corner, up the next flight of stairs, or on the next page.

Terrorism carries this sense of menace from an existential to a political level. Two episodes of terrorism occur in the text. The first has to do with Ulrich's father's involvement in the abortive plot against Hitler. The second has to do with the Einzieh Group, responsible for arson, assault, kidnapping, armed robbery, first- and second-degree murder, and various bombings, and its being avenged by the Seventh of June Liberation Group, which plants twelve sticks of dynamite in the post office Helmut designed. The group's second bomb destroys the police station Helmut designed, and the third partially destroys a drawbridge in Ganzlich after Gottfried, the drawbridge operator whom the terrorists convert, kills two policemen. The terrorist group "applauded the heroic action of [this] German worker who, on his own initiative, forcefully expressed his rejection of a system of government in which the worker is kept in permanent bondage" (248). They neglect to mention, however, that they have coerced Gottfried into doing what he did, that he has simply replaced one less deadly system of bondage with another more deadly one, and that "the two policemen killed . . . also were working class, as were the fishermen whose boats were now prevented from reaching the North Sea" (248).

Political terrorism becomes an analogue for literary deconstructionism. Both seek to undermine the dominant value systems. Both seek to present a culture with its opposite, thereby uncovering what a culture must believe in order to exist. And both use a kind of violence as their means to an end—the former's is physical, the latter's interpretive. In the text, Abish's "great outrage" (40) at both is clear, despite his claim elsewhere that "both are open to interpretation" (Lotringer 6). To put it another way, both might be open to interpretation, but the kind of interpretaton to which they are open centers, as similar questions did in *The White Hotel,* on moral and historical questions—on totalizing systems.

As a consequence, Abish forges a link between Ulrich's individual trauma and Germany's national one. Ulrich feels dislocated as "a prisoner of the present" (*How German Is It* 54). The result is that he turns toward the past in his search for stability. He tries to convince himself that he is the son of Ulrich von Hargenau, who, he claims, was executed for his role in the assassination attempt on Hitler. He tries to convince himself that he is the offspring of a man associated with morality at the most immoral point in German history. In fact, he realizes early in his life that "I had been born too long after my father's imprisonment and execution for me to be his son." So, as Ulrich says, he practices "a sort of self-deception. I still don't have the slightest cue as to who my father could be . . . and I almost prefer it that way, prefer it to discovering that my father was someone in the Einsatzkommando" (250). Ulrich deceives himself about the past in his desire for a compensatory present but ultimately finds himself implicated like all other young Germans in his country's guilt.

In the same way, Germany as a whole deceives itself about the past in its desire for a compensatory present. As the novel begins, the narrator asks what the first thing visitors to Germany would notice about the country. In addition to the "painstaking cleanliness" and "all-pervasive sense of order," he answers, there would be "the new striking architecture." Contemporary fifteen- and twenty-story buildings covered with glass reflect "not only the sky but also . . . the older historical sites, those clusters of carefully reconstructed buildings that are an attempt to replicate entire neighborhoods obliterated during the last war" (2–3). As with the narrative itself, the new contains the old within itself. The present apparent perfection contains within itself the potential for past atrocities. Beneath the seeming prosperity and well-being of Brumholdstein lie the bodies that could be the inmates of the Durst concentration camp or the Germans killed by those inmates upon their release (192). Abish goes out of his way to emphasize that this phenomenon is not particular to Germany and that it would therefore be wrong simply to pass such a discovery off as one more example of "the image of the Germans as collectively dangerous and destructive" (4). Rather, "it could happen anywhere else—this smooth and agreeable surface broken by . . . an unexpected violence" (3). Germans "have come to resemble all other stable, postindustrial, technologically advanced nations" (4), and perhaps this is the most frightening realization of all.

Abish uses Brumhold, "who is really Heidegger" (Lotringer 5), to raise two contradictory points. The first is that language is at worst self-referential, at best an oblique mirror of the world; this is a purely postmodern point. The second is a purely anti-postmodern point having to do with the echoes behind Heidegger of "his questionable political role in the thirties" (4), of political and ethical questions. Again it seems all well and good to discuss in abstract terms the ironies and failures of language, but behind such surface concerns lies the overpowering and unpalatable existential-historical truth of the extermination of twelve million people, six million of whom were Jews. A double logic arises in the text, each side of which exists only by exclusion of the other. The creation of a highly artificial self-reflexive literary structure has absolutely nothing to do with the very real hyperbarbarism of the Nazi atrocities, or, for that matter, Vietnam, nuclear war, or any of the other many horrors in the second half of the twentieth century. It is one thing to realize that signs are signs, and that some of them are lies. It is another thing entirely to realize what Walter Reich noted at a conference gathering survivors of the Holocaust: "it was reality that drove out the theory when, in the midst of [excessive psychological theorizing], videotaped interviews from the archives of the Holocaust Survivors Film Project were shown, interviews of survivors talking not about Freud but about the black and lifeless sun of Auschwitz" (23).

Christa McAuliffe as Icarus

Abish's comments, in spite of his misleading extratextual comments, seem to place him firmly in the tradition of such diverse politically and ethically conscious writers as Zola, Dreiser, and Camus. That is, at the stratum of content we apparently find a positive drive toward the reinterpretation and correction of human systems by means of a humanist art. We uncover a drive that seemingly affirms our belief in the shared speech, the shared values, and the shared perception that, we would like to believe, form our culture. In this way, Abish appears to enter into the mode of consciousness that attempts to assert centrism and closure. We apparently have reached once more in literary history a Sartrean sense of engagement where humanity has been reactivated, where "in choosing for himself [man] chooses for all men" (Sartre 350), and where the human, the cultural, and the ironic have resurfaced.

The image of Ulrich in particular and Germany in general yearning for a stable past in the midst of a disjunctive present is an analogue for *How German Is It* itself, for the first turns away from postmodernity and toward a neoconservatism. The content of the text expresses a longing for centrism that its form seems to dismantle. Consequently, Abish's novel serves as an example of an apparently new trend in contemporary theory and literature that points to the crisis of what has come to be called postmodernity.

Caramello first argued as much with respect to American fiction by writers such as Gass, Barth, Federman, and Gangemi, who in their projects display a certain hesitation between Barthes's notion of "work" and "text" and Derrida's of "book" and "writing." Both "work" and "book," on the one hand, express "the idea of a totality" or a belief in a transcendental signified. "Text" and "writing," on the other, are forms of disruption and "aphoristic energy" that stand opposed to the notion of "work" and "book" (*Of Grammatology* 18). The "work" and "book" embody the possibility of a metanarrative, while "text" and "writing" embody freeplay that undoes the possibility of a metanarrative. In American postmodern fiction, Caramello asserts, a yearning exists "for the book and the self that (its) writing has dismembered" (35). A similar point has recently been made by John McGowan, who argues the presence of the same kind of tension between absolutism and pluralism in the postmodern theories of Jameson, Derrida, and Foucault. McGowan concludes that "I think it fair to say that postmodernists want pluralism, but believe deep down (or, at the very least, are sorely afraid) that society and discourse are, in fact, monolithic" (12).

How German Is It seems part of a larger destabilization that until a short time ago went unnoticed. Perhaps this destabilization has in fact been at the margins of the postmodern since its inception, as Caramello seems to suggest through his choice of examples. Perhaps it is something new, as I read it—an attempt either at reconciliation with the modern and premodern or a sign of the first push beyond the postmodern. At most, this new sense of destabilization subverts the postmodern via its traditional concerns; it perverts the notion of polyphonics via its monologic patterns. At least, we can say that critics have begun reading the interior of the postmodern as evincing a certain nostalgia for a past that never existed, a nostalgia that has taken the first step toward the deconstruction of its own exterior. And with such a sense of nostalgia (found in the works of writers such as Mason, Carver, and Beattie) the humorous vision perhaps begins its return to the margins of discourse and to a stabilized state where gravity will reassert itself so that our culture once again will emphasize the pathos of Christa McAuliffe's Icarian fall—the circus of the mind in motion will once again give way to irony for what has vanished—and things will try once again to find their final places.

9.
Afterburn

It's the end of the world as we know it (and
I feel fine).
—R.E.M., *Document*

Three years before the fact, the filmmaker
Godfrey Reggio prophesied the image of the Challenger turning into
a fireball and killing all seven crew members on board. In the penultimate sequence of *Koyaanisqatsi,* whose title comes from the Hopi,
suggesting *"life out of balance,"* we see, in slow-motion, a rocket ease
off its launchpad and dazzlingly ascend into an electric blue sky. It
rises powerfully and beatifically, and, just as it is about to free itself
from Earth's atmosphere, just as it is about to take that magical
quantum leap into the absolute freedom of space, it explodes, turns
into a churning yellow cloud. The camera locks onto part of a booster
as it leisurely spins in circles out of the sky, an occasional flame
licking from its interior. The image, of course, takes us back once
more to Icarus, who tempted fate by flying too close to the sun. It
could also serve as a beautiful emblem of postmodernity itself, strain-
ing for release from the gravity of reason and mimesis, imploding into
the black hole of its own contradictions and limitations, and finally
falling from grace as our culture's dominant mode of consciousness.

This book, which has attempted to sketch that hypothetical
trajectory—that gravity's rainbow—has itself turned out finally to be
a kind of Janus-text. On the one hand, it has clearly delighted in the
polymorphous perversity of the postmodern enterprise, embraced a
humorous paradigm of reading that teases texts to speak in dialects

146

their authors did not intend. Surely, this is the case, for instance, with my reading of Burgess's *A Clockwork Orange* and Abish's *How German Is It.* It has delighted in postmodern humor's bliss in the proliferation of micronarratives, in radical skepticism, in polyphony. On the other hand, and paradoxically, it has clearly been wary of the schizophrenic impulse in the postmodern enterprise and has embraced an ironic paradigm of reading that looks below the freeplay of surfaces in an attempt to retrieve some golden meaning. Surely, this is the case with my readings of Davenport's *Da Vinci's Bicycle* and D. M. Thomas's *The White Hotel.* This book has embraced modernism's belief in the power of art—and criticism—to make cosmos out of chaos. As with texts such as *Lolita* or *The White Hotel,* then, my book, *Circus of the Mind,* stutters between extremes on the modern-postmodern continuum. It walks a theoretical tightrope. By doing so, it exposes its own deeply ambivalent premises about the humorous radicalism of postmodernity and the ironic conservatism of the neorealism that apparently has come to replace it. To this extent, it has become a register of the decade in which it was composed. It has become, like all critical texts, time-locked.

Throughout the course of its argument, *Circus* has been keenly aware that it is working in the realm of theory, that theory is good but that it doesn't prevent things from happening. We draw road maps so that we don't get lost. But, as we try to follow them, we inevitably understand that road maps are road maps, not the highways to which they hope to point. We cannot drive *on* them but must drive *with* them, and, very often, we must drive *in spite* of them. When attempting to chart postmodernity, many mappers cannot even agree on whether we are plotting Louisville or Laghouat, whether we are using the same symbols with which to plot, whether we even agree on what road maps are. To put it simply, my road map will likely be very different from others. If I used different-colored pens (more of the new critical or biographical and less of the sociohistorical or reader-responsive, for instance), or if I plotted other lands (the texts of Alexander Theroux, Thomas McGuane, and John Updike perhaps), chances are that I would indeed have ended up mapping very different interstates than I did. I am comfortable with the notion that the map I have constructed has at least rendered each of the highways it examined a little more interesting and a little more comprehensible than it was before—and that, it seems to me, is a fine goal for a map.

Humans—even postmodern ones, for better or worse—are patternmakers, and the patterns I have made follow what I perceive to be the rise and fall of postmodernity and its essentially humorous vision. If the premodern attitude embraces the idea of a metanarrative, and the modern *seeks* to embrace it, then the postmodern basks in the proliferation of micronarratives. It holds itself in opposition to all that is static, and it attempts to decenter, detotalize, and demythologize while taking nothing, including its own (non)premises, very seriously. In this way, postmodernity interrogates all we once took for granted about language and experience. It is easy to see that such a perspective jibes nicely with the comic vision, whose goal is to topple the authority of any monologic view and delight in the infinite freeplay of polyphony and plurality—a circus of the mind in motion. As opposed to modern irony and premodern "seriousness" (for wont of a better word), postmodern humor focuses on question rather than answer, process rather than goal.

Postmodern humor is not an historical period, but an attitude, and in our culture it came to dominance for a relatively brief time. Though one can surely find such an attitude at least as far back as Cervantes, if not Petronius, and though at the outset of our own century one can surely hear its discord sounding in the work of creators such as Kafka and Duchamp, it surfaced with a vengeance shortly after the Second World War in the absurdist impulse, flowered in the 1960s and first half of the 1970s and began to become marginalized once again in the late 1970s and 1980s. Guy Davenport's project, for the purposes of this book, has become emblematic of the modern, of the renaissance of the archaic, of the metanarrative that embraces Art and the Great Tradition. Opposed to this are Vladimir Nabokov's *Lolita* and Anthony Burgess's *A Clockwork Orange*. Both of these fictions, each in its own way, teeter between the modern and postmodern and, hence, become emblematic of a kind of Janus-text that flourished in the late 1950s and early 1960s as postmodernity began its move toward dominance.

If Davenport is the quintessential modern ironist, then Samuel Beckett in a text such as *How It Is* and Barthelme in all his projects are the quintessential postmodern humorists. Beckett's text turns joking against itself and its readers, the last centers of authority, while Barthelme's texts turn language itself into a kind of slapstick routine. The works of these fiction writers come to stand for a kind of text that has, in the 1960s and first half of the 1970s, turned the pluriverse into a gag. They agree with John Self, the protagonist of Martin Amis's novel, *Money,* when he argues that "I'll always be the guy in the joke. . . . It's the twentieth-century feeling. We're the jokes. . . . You just got to live the joke" (270).

Finally, D. M. Thomas's *White Hotel* and Walter Abish's *How*

German Is It represent the kind of text produced in the late 1970s and 1980s that has moved through the blast furnace of postmodernity and been transformed. These are texts that both try to buy into the basic orthodoxy of postmodernity, in terms of its aesthetics, and try to interrogate that orthodoxy in terms of its politics and metaphysics. These two novels represent the first moves away from pure postmodernity, hence again taking the form of Janus-texts.

As I was working on the last lines of this book, a student of mine brought a recent issue of *Spy* magazine to my attention. In it appears a satiric article by Bruce Handy called "Post-Postmodernism." While the piece itself is a kind of joke, a general attack on trendiness, the heart of its message is indicative of our culture's move away from "PoMo." Handy catalogues the frequency of the use of the term *postmodern* from 1980 to 1987 in a number of important American newspapers, including the *New York Times,* the *Washington Post,* and the *Los Angeles Times.* In 1980 there were twenty-one appearances of the term. By 1987 there were 247. More interesting, according to Handy, is that those using the word *postmodern* had no idea what they meant by it. *Postmodern,* Handy concludes:

> has less and less to do with *any* kind of art; it's evolved into the sort of buzzword that people tack onto sentences when they're trying to sound more educated than they fear they really are, not unlike the way *gestalt* was used in the 1970s, or *science* in the Dark Ages. Now we read about postmodern politicians grappling with postmodern economics while postmodern talk shows discuss postmodern sex. (102)

Handy goes on to give tongue-in-cheek menus for PoMo architecture ("Does the building have pilasters or pediments or the same color scheme as the 1984 Summer Olympics?"), music ("Does the piece make use of old TV themes or Malcolm X speeches?"), painting ("Does the work combine naked figures and old advertising characters in a cryptic, arbitrary manner?"), television ("Do the characters talk to the camera sometimes?"), and cuisine ("Does it have a purplish element?"). His gesture marks the end of the world as we know it. His gesture marks the beginning of something perhaps as yet "unnamable."

This, at least from the point of view of my own myopia, tends to be the way literary history works. The dominance of conservative attitudes oscillate with the dominance of subversive attitudes. The Neoclassical is subverted by the Romantic, the Romantic by the Victorian, the Victorian by the Modern. Now, apparently, the radicalism of the postmodern has given way to the conservatism of neorealism. As we approach the last decade of the last century of this millennium, the oscillations seem to have become more rapid but the same basic pattern still exists. If we project the pattern into the future, it suggests that we will see a new subversion arise in the arts once again at the end of our century and the beginning of the next, just as the arts did at the end of the nineteenth and beginning of the twentieth. A culture that perceives itself as undergoing crisis will produce artifacts of crisis. A culture that perceives itself as content with its premises will produce artifacts of conservatism. The rise in this last decade of neorealism has perhaps then signaled nothing very new at all. Rather, it might simply be a common human reaction to the radically subversive, a tentative and limited answer to a state of *koyaanisqatsi,* to a way of life that calls for another way of living.

Bibliography

Primary Works

Abish, Walter. *How German Is It.* New York: New Directions, 1980.
———. *In the Future Perfect.* New York: New Directions, 1977.
Amis, Martin. *Money.* New York: Penguin, 1986.
Barthelme, Donald. *The Dead Father.* New York: Pocket, 1975.
———. *Snow White.* New York: Bantam Books, 1971.
———. *Sixty Stories.* New York: G. P. Putnam's, 1981.
———. *Unspeakable Practices, Unnatural Acts.* New York: Farrar, 1968.
Beckett, Samuel. *Endgame.* New York: Grove, 1958.
———. *How It Is.* New York: Grove, 1964.
Berio, Luciano. Jacket notes for "Visage." *Electronic Music.* Turnabout-Vox. No catalog number, n.d.
Borges, Jorge Luis. *Ficciones.* Tr. Alastair Reid et al. New York: Grove, 1962.
———. *Labyrinths.* Ed. Donald A. Yates and James E. Irby. New York: New Directions, 1964.
Burgess, Anthony. *A Clockwork Orange.* New York: Norton, 1963.
———. *A Clockwork Orange.* New York: Norton, 1987.
———. "*A Clockwork Orange:* The Missing Chapter." *Rolling Stone* (26 March 1987): 74–80.
Davenport, Guy. *Da Vinci's Bicycle: Ten Stories by Guy Davenport.* Baltimore: Johns Hopkins UP, 1979.
DeLillo, Don. *White Noise.* New York: Penguin, 1985.
Heller, Joseph. *Catch-22.* New York: Dell, 1979.
Lodge, David. *Small World: An Academic Romance.* New York: Penguin, 1985.
Nabokov, Vladimir. *The Annotated Lolita.* Ed. Alfred Appel, Jr. New York: McGraw, 1970.
Pynchon, Thomas. *The Crying of Lot 49.* New York: Bantam, 1966.
———. *Gravity's Rainbow.* New York: Viking, 1973.

————. *V.* New York: Bantam, 1963.

Stendhal [Henri Beyle]. *The Red and the Black.* Trans. Lloyd C. Parks. New York: NAL, 1970.

Sukenick, Ronald. *98.6.* New York: Fiction Collective, 1975.

Thomas, D. M. *The White Hotel.* New York: Pocket, 1982.

Vonnegut, Kurt. *Breakfast of Champions.* New York: Delacorte, 1973.

Yeats, W. B. "Meditations in Time of Civil War." *The Poems of W. B. Yeats.* Ed. Richard J. Finneran. New York: Macmillan, 1983.

Secondary Works

In addition to being a list of secondary works cited, the following is a selected bibliography of postmodernism and humor. Such a bibliography is bound to be both incomplete and filled with a number of implicit judgments and decisions, but throughout I have tried to keep the student in mind and have covered what I feel are the major works in each area.

Aggeler, Geoffrey, ed. *Critical Essays on Anthony Burgess.* Boston: Hall, 1986.

Allsop, Kenneth. "Those American Sickniks." *Twentieth Century* 170 (1961): 97–101.

Alter, Robert. "Mimesis and the Motive for Fiction." *TriQuarterly* 42 (1978): 233.

————. *Partial Magic: The Novel as Self-Conscious Genre.* Berkeley: U California P, 1975.

Amis, Kingsley. "She Was a Child and I Was a Child." *Spectator* 6 Nov. 1959: 633–36.

Anderson, Donald. "Comic Modes in American Fiction." *Southern Review: An Australian Journal of Literary Studies* 8 (1975): 549–60.

Appel, Alfred, Jr. "An Interview with Vladimir Nabokov." Dembo 19–44.

————. Introduction. *The Annotated* Lolita. xv–lxxvi.

————. "*Lolita:* The Springboard for Parody." Dembo 106–43.

Arac, Jonathan, ed. *Postmodernism and Politics: New Directions.* Minneapolis: U Minnesota P, 1986.

Aristotle. "Poetics." *Critical Theory Since Plato.* Ed. Hazard Adams. New York: Harcourt, 1971. 47–66.

Baillet, Whitney. *New Yorker* 21 Dec. 1981.

Bain, Alexander. *The Emotions and the Will.* London: Parker, 1859.

————. "Wit and Humour." *Westminster Review* 48 (1847): 47–59.

Bair, Deirdre. *Samuel Beckett.* New York: Harcourt, 1978.

Bakhtin, Mikhail. *Problems of Dostoevsky's Poetics.* Ed. and tr. Caryl Emerson. Minneapolis: U Minnesota P, 1984.

Barth, John. "The Literature of Exhaustion." *Atlantic Monthly* Aug. 1967: 29–34.

———. "The Literature of Replenishment: Postmodern Fiction." *Atlantic Monthly* Jan. 1980: 65–71.

Barthelme, Donald. "Symposium on Fiction." *Shenandoah* 27.2 (1976): 3–31.

Barthes, Roland. "The Death of the Author." *Image-Music-Text.* Tr. Stephen Heath. New York: Hill and Wang, 1977.

———. "From Work to Text." *Image-Music-Text.* Tr. Stephen Heath. New York: Hill and Wang, 1977.

———. *Writing Degree Zero.* Tr. Annette Lavers and Colin Smith. New York: Hill, 1983.

Baudrillard, Jean. "The Ecstasy of Communication." *The Anti-Aesthetic: Essays on Postmodern Culture.* Ed. Hal Foster. Port Townsend: Bay, 1983.

Bell, Daniel. *The Cultural Contradictions of Capitalism.* New York: Basic, 1976.

Benamou, Michel, and Charles Caramello, eds. *Performance in Postmodern Culture.* Madison: Coda, 1977.

Bergson, Henri. "Laughter." *Comedy.* Ed. Wylie Sypher. Garden City: Doubleday, 1956. 60–190.

Berio, Luciano. Jacket notes for "Visage." *Electronic Music.* Turnabout-Vox. No catalog number, n.d.

Bernstein, Richard J., ed. *Habermas and Modernity.* Cambridge: MIT P, 1985.

Blair, Walter. "Aftermath: Twentieth-Century Humorists." *Native American Humor.* San Francisco: Chandler, 1960.

Blau, Herbert. *The Eye of Prey: Subversions of the Postmodern.* Bloomington: Indiana UP, 1987.

Blistein, Elmer. *Comedy in Action.* Durham: Duke UP, 1964.

Bloom, Harold. *The Anxiety of Influence: A Theory of Poetry.* New York: Oxford UP, 1975.

———. *A Map of Misreading.* New York: Oxford UP, 1975.

Booth, Wayne C. *The Rhetoric of Fiction.* Chicago: U Chicago P, 1961.

———. *A Rhetoric of Irony.* Chicago: U Chicago P, 1974.

Bradbury, Malcolm, and James McFarlane, eds. *Modernism: 1890–1930.* London: Penguin, 1976.

Brown, Lady Falls. "*The White Hotel:* D. M. Thomas's Considerable Debt to Anatoli Kuznetsov and *Babi Yar.*" *South Central Review* 2.2 (1985):60–79.

Brustein, Robert. "The Healthiness of Sick Comedy." *New Republic* 15 Dec. 1962: 28–30.

Burford, Bill. Editorial. *Granta* 8 (1983): 4–5.

Burgess, Anthony. "Alex on Today's Youth: Creeching Golosses and Filthy Toofles!" *New York Times Book Review* 31 May 1987: 7,18.

———. *1985*. Boston: Little, Brown, 1978.

———. *Re Joyce*. New York: Ballantine, 1966.

Burgin, Victor. *The End of Art Theory: Criticism and Postmodernity*. Atlantic Highlands, NJ: Humanities Press International, 1986.

Butler, Christopher. *After the Wake: An Essay on the Contemporary Avant-Garde*. Oxford: Clarendon, 1980.

Butler, Diana. "*Lolita* Lepidoptera." *New World Writing* 16. Philadelphia: Lippincott, 1960. 58–64.

Caputi, Anthony. *Buffo: The Genius of Vulgar Comedy*. Detroit: Wayne State UP, 1978.

Caramello, Charles. *Silverless Mirrors: Book, Self and Postmodern American Fiction*. Tallahassee: UP Florida, 1983.

Charney, Maurice. *Comedy High and Low*. New York: Oxford UP, 1978.

Chase, Richard. *The American Novel and Its Tradition*. Baltimore: Johns Hopkins UP, 1957.

Chatman, Seymour. *Story and Discourse: Narrative Structure in Fiction and Film*. Ithaca: Cornell UP, 1978.

Churchill, Thomas. "An Interview with Anthony Burgess." *Malahat Review* 17 (1971): 103–27.

Cixous, Hélène. "La fiction et ses fantômes: Une lecture de l'*Unheimliche* de Freud." *Poétique* 10 (1973): 199–216.

Cohen, Sarah Blacher, ed. *Comic Relief: Humor in Contemporary American Literature*. Urbana: U Illinois P, 1978.

Cohn, Ruby, ed. *Samuel Beckett: A Collection of Criticism Edited by Ruby Cohn*. New York: McGraw, 1975.

Cook, Albert. *The Dark Voyage and the Golden Mean: A Philosophy of Comedy*. Cambridge: Harvard UP, 1949.

Corrigan, Robert W., ed. *Comedy: Meaning and Form*. New York: Harper, 1981.

"Davenport, Guy." *Contemporary Authors: A Bio-Bibliographical Guide to Current Authors and Their Works*. Detroit: Gale, 1978. Vols. 33–36.

Davenport, Guy. *Every Force Evolves a Form*. San Francisco: North Point, 1987.

———. *The Geography of the Imagination*. San Francisco: North Point, 1981.

Dearlove, J. E. "The Voice and Its Words: 'How It Is.' " *On Beckett: Essays and Criticism*. Ed. S. E. Gontarski. New York: Grove, 1986.

de Man, Paul. *Allegories of Reading: Figural Language in the Rhetoric of Contemporary Criticism*. New York: Oxford UP, 1971.

Dembo, L. S., ed. *Nabokov: The Man and His Work*. Madison: U Wisconsin P, 1967.

DeMott, Benjamin. "The New Irony: Sickniks and Others." *American Scholar* 31 (1961–62): 108–19.

Derrida, Jacques. *Of Grammatology*. Tr. Gayatri Chakravorty Spivak. Baltimore: Johns Hopkins UP, 1976.

———. *Margins of Philosophy*. Tr. Alan Bass. Chicago: U Chicago P, 1982.

———. "Structure, Sign, and Play in the Discourse of the Human Sciences." *The Structuralist Controversy*. Ed. Richard Macksey and Eugenio Donato. Baltimore: Johns Hopkins UP, 1972. 247–72.

Donoghue, Denis. "The Promiscuous Cool of Postmodernism." *New York Times Book Review* 22 June 1986: 1, 37–38.

Dubois, Arthur F. "Poe and *Lolita*." *CEA Critic* 26.6 (1964): 1, 7.

Eastman, Max. *The Sense of Humor*. New York: Scribners, 1922.

Eco, Umberto. "Towards a New Middle Ages." *On Signs*. Ed. Marshall Blonsky. Baltimore: Johns Hopkins UP, 1985: 488–504.

Elgin, Don D. "The Comedy of Fantasy: An Ecological Perspective of Joy Chant's *Red Moon and Black Mountain*." *Aspects of Fantasy: Selected Essays from the Second International Conference on the Fantastic in Literature and Film*. Ed. William Coyle. Wesport: Greenwood, 1986. 221–30.

Eliot, T. S. "*Ulysses,* Order, and Myth." *Dial* 75 (1923): 480–83.

Esslin, Martin. *The Theatre of the Absurd*. New York: Penguin, 1980.

Falkenberg, Betty. "Literary Games." *New York Times Book Review* 4 January 1981.

Federman, Raymond. "Imagination as Plagiarism [an unfinished paper . . .]." *New Literary History* 7 (1976): 563–78.

Feibleman, James. *In Praise of Comedy*. New York: Horizon, 1970.

Fiedler, Leslie. "The New Mutants." *Partisan Review* 32 (1965): 505–25.

Fokkema, Douwe. *Literary History, Modernism, and Postmodernism*. Philadelphia: J. Benjamins, 1984.

Foster, Hal, ed. *The Anti-Aesthetic: Essays on Postmodern Culture*. Port Townsend: Bay, 1983.

Foucault, Michel. *The Order of Things: An Archeology of the Human Sciences*. New York: Pantheon, 1970.

Freud, Sigmund. *An Outline of Psycho-Analysis*. Tr. and ed. James Strachey. New York: Norton, 1949.

———. "Wit and Its Relation to the Unconscious." *The Basic Writings of Sigmund Freud*. Tr. and ed. A. A. Brill. New York: Modern Library, 1938. 633–803.

Frohock, W. M. "The Edge of Laughter: Some Modern Fiction and the Grotesque." *Veins of Humor*. Ed. Harry Levin. Cambridge: Harvard UP, 1972.

Frye, Northrop. *Anatomy of Criticism: Four Essays*. Princeton: Princeton UP, 1957.

Gaggi, Silvio. *Modern/Postmodern: A Study in Twentieth-Century Arts and Ideas*. Philadelphia: U Pennsylvania P, 1989.

Galligan, Edward L. *The Comic Vision in Literature*. Athens: U Georgia P, 1984.

Garvin, Harry R., ed. *Romanticism, Modernism, Postmodernism*. Lewisburg: Bucknell UP, 1980.

Gass, William. "The Death of the Author." *Salmagundi* 65 (1984): 3–26.

―――. *Habitations of the Word: Essays*. New York: Simon, 1985.

Gontarski, S. E., ed. *On Beckett: Essays and Criticism*. New York: Grove, 1986.

Graff, Gerald. *Literature Against Itself: Literary Ideas in Modern Society*. Chicago: U Chicago P, 1979.

Greenberg, Clement. "Modern and Postmodern." *Arts Magazine* 54 (1980): 64–66.

Gurewitch, Morton. *Comedy: The Irrational Vision*. Ithaca: Cornell UP, 1975.

Gwynn, Frederick L., and Joseph L. Blotner, eds. *Faulkner in the University: Class Conferences at the University of Virginia*. Charlottesville: U Virginia P, 1959.

Hall, James. *The Tragic Comedians*. Bloomington: Indiana UP, 1963.

Handy, Bruce. "Post-Postmodernism." *Spy* Apr. 1988: 100–108.

Harari, Josué V., ed. *Textual Strategies: Perspectives in Post-Structuralist Criticism*. Ithaca: Cornell UP, 1979.

Harris, Charles B. *Contemporary American Novelists of the Absurd*. New Haven: College and UP, 1971.

Hartman, Geoffrey H. *Criticism in the Wilderness: The Study of Literature Today*. New Haven: Yale UP, 1980.

Hassan, Ihab. *The Dismemberment of Orpheus*. 2nd ed. Madison: U Wisconsin P, 1982.

―――. *Paracriticisms*. Urbana: U Illinois P, 1975.

―――. *The Postmodern Turn: Essay in Postmodern Theory and Culture*. Ohio State UP, 1987.

―――, and Sally Hassan, ed. *Innovation/Renovation: New Perspectives on the Humanities*. Madison: U Wisconsin P, 1983.

Hatch, Robert. "Films." *Nation* 23 June 1962: 563–64.

Heidegger, Martin. *Poetry, Language, Thought*. Tr. Albert Hofstadter. New York: Harper, 1971.

Heilman, Robert. *The Ways of the World: Comedy and Society*. Seattle: U Washington P, 1978.

Heisenberg, Werner. *Physics and Beyond: Encounters and Conversations*. Tr. Arnold J. Pomerans. New York: Harper, 1971.

Hicks, Granville. "Lolita and Her Problems." *Saturday Review* 16 Aug. 1958: 12, 38.

Hoffmann, Peter. *The History of the German Resistance 1933–1945.* Cambridge: MIT P, 1977.

Holden, Jonathan. *Style and Authenticity in Postmodern Poetry.* Columbia: U Missouri P, 1986.

Holland, Norman. "Postmodern Psychoanalysis." Hassan, *Innovation / Renovation.*

Hollander, John. Rev. of *Lolita. Partisan Review* 23 (1956): 557–60.

Howe, Irving. "Mass Society and Post-Modern Fiction." *Partisan Review* 26 (1959): 420–36.

Hughes, Riley. "New Books." *Catholic World* Oct. 1958: 72.

Huis, Mary Ellen. *Postmodernism: A Bibliography.* Monticello: Vance Bibliographies, 1985.

Huizinga, Johan. *Homo Ludens: A Study of the Play-Element in Culture.* N. trans. Boston: Beacon, 1955.

Hume, Kathryn. *Fantasy and Mimesis: Responses to Reality in Western Literature.* New York: Methuen, 1984.

———. *Pynchon's Mythography: An Approach to* Gravity's Rainbow. Carbondale: Southern Illinois UP, 1987.

Hutcheon, Linda. *Narcissistic Narrative: The Metafictional Paradox.* Waterloo: Wilfrid Laurier UP, 1980.

———. *A Poetics of Postmodernism: History, Theory, Fiction.* New York: Routledge, 1988.

Huyssen, Andreas. *After the Great Divide: Modernism, Mass Culture, Postmodernism.* Bloomington: Indiana UP, 1986.

Iser, Wolfgang. *The Implied Reader: Patterns of Communication in Prose Fiction from Bunyan to Beckett.* Baltimore: Johns Hopkins U P, 1974.

Jackson, Rosemary. *Fantasy: The Literature of Subversion.* New York: Methuen, 1981.

James, William. *Pragmatism and Four Essays from The Meaning of Truth.* New York: NAL, 1974.

Jameson, Fredric. "Metacommentary." *PMLA* 86 (1971): 9–17.

———. "Postmodernism and Consumer Society." Foster, 111–25.

Jencks, Charles, ed. *The Language of Postmodern Architecture.* New York: Rizzoli, 1984.

Kant, Immanuel. *Critique of Judgement.* Tr. J. H. Bernard. New York: Hafner, 1951.

Karl, Frederick R. *American Fictions 1940–1980.* New York: Harper, 1983.

Kennard, Jean E. *Number and Nightmare: Forms of Fantasy in Contemporary Fiction.* Hamden: Archon, 1975.

Kenner, Hugh. *The Pound Era.* Berkeley: U California P, 1971.

———. *Samuel Beckett: A Critical Study.* Berkeley: U California P, 1968.

Kermode, Frank. *The Sense of an Ending: Studies in the Theory of Fiction.* New York: Oxford UP, 1967.

Klinkowitz, Jerome. "A Final Word for Black Humor." *Contemporary Literature* 15 (1974): 271–76.

————. *Literary Disruptions: The Making of a Post-Contemporary American Fiction.* Urbana: U Illinois P, 1984.

————. "Walter Abish and the Surfaces of Life." *Georgia Review* 35 (1981): 416–20.

Knowlton, James. "How German Is It?" *American Book Review* 3.3 (1981).

Kristeva, Julia. "The Pain and Sorrow of the Modern World: The Works of Marguerite Duras." *PMLA* 102.2 (1987): 138–52.

Kroker, Arthur, and David Cook. *The Postmodern Scene: Excremental Culture and Hyper-Aesthetics.* New York: St. Martins, 1986.

Kuznetsov, Anatoli. *Babi Yar.* New York: Dell, 1967.

Lang, Candace D. *Irony / Humor: Critical Paradigms.* Baltimore: Johns Hopkins UP, 1988.

Langbaum, Robert. *The Mysteries of Identity: A Theme in Modern Literature.* Chicago: U Chicago P, 1977.

Lauter, Paul, ed. *Theories of Comedy.* Garden City: Doubleday, 1953.

Leacock, Stephen. *Humor: Its Theory and Technique.* London: Lane, 1935.

Lentricchia, Frank. *After the New Criticism.* Chicago: U Chicago P, 1980.

Levin, Harry. "What Was Modernism?" *Massachusetts Review* 1.4 (1960): 609–30.

Lévi-Strauss, Claude. *The Raw and the Cooked.* Tr. John Weightman and Doreen Weightman. New York: Harper, 1970.

Lodge, David. *The Modes of Modern Writing: Metaphor, Metonymy, and the Typology of Modern Literature.* London: Edward Arnold, 1977.

Lotringer, Sylvère. "Walter Abish: *Wie Deutsch Ist Es.*" *Semiotext(e)* 4.2 (1985): 1–9.

Ludovici, Anthony. *The Secret of Laughter.* London: Constable, 1932.

Lukács, Georg. *The Theory of the Novel: A Historico-Philosophical Essay on the Forms of Great Epic Literature.* Tr. Anna Bostock. Cambridge: MIT P, 1971.

Lutwack, Leonard. "Mixed and Uniform Prose Styles in the Novel." *Theory of the Novel.* Ed. Philip Stevick. New York: Free, 1967.

Lynch, William. *Christ and Apollo: The Dimensions of the Literary Imagination.* New York: Sheed, 1960.

Lyotard, Jean-François. *The Postmodern Condition.* Tr. Geoff Bennington and Brian Massumi. Minneapolis: U Minnesota P, 1984.

———— and Jean-Loup Thébaud. *Just Gaming.* Tr. Wlad Godzich. Minneapolis: U Minnesota P, 1985.

McCaffery, Larry. *Postmodern Fiction: A Bio-Bibliographical Guide.* Westport: Greenwood, 1986.

————, and Sinda Gregory. *Alive and Writing: Interviews with American Authors in the 1980s.* Urbana: U Illinois P, 1987.

McFadden, George. *Discovering the Comic.* Princeton: Princeton UP, 1982.

McGowan, John. "Postmodᵤnism and its Discontents." MLA Convention. New York, 1986.

McHale, Brian. "Modernist Reading, Post-Modern Text: The Case of *Gravity's Rainbow.*" *Poetics Today* 1 (1979): 85–110.

————. *Postmodernist Fiction.* New York: Methuen, 1987.

McMillan, Dougald. "Samuel Beckett and the Visual Arts: The Embarrassment of Allegory." *On Beckett: Essays and Criticism.* Ed. S. E. Gontarski. New York: Grove, 1986.

Malin, Irving. "In So Many Words." *Ontario Review* 9 (1978–79): 112–14.

Mazzaro, Jerome. *Postmodern American Poetry.* Urbana: U Illinois P, 1980.

Meeker, Joseph. *The Comedy of Survival: Studies in Literary Ecology.* New York: Scribner, 1974.

Mercier, Vivian. *The New Novel from Queneau to Pinget.* New York: Farrar, 1971.

Merivale, Patricia. "The Flaunting of Artifice in Vladimir Nabokov and Jorge Luis Borges." Dembo 209–24.

Monro, D. H. "Humor." *The Encyclopedia of Philosophy.* New York: Macmillan and Free, 1967: 90–93.

Morace, Robert A. "Invention in Guy Davenport's *Da Vinci's Bicycle.*" *Critique: Studies in Modern Fiction* 22.3 (1981): 71–87.

Morris, Robert K. *The Consolations of Ambiguity: An Essay on the Novels of Anthony Burgess.* Columbia: U Missouri P, 1971.

Nabokov, Vladimir. *Lectures on Literature.* Ed. Fredson Bowers. New York: Harcourt, 1980.

————. *Strong Opinions.* New York: McGraw, 1973.

Nemerov, Howard. "The Morality of Art." *Kenyon Review* 19 (1957): 313–21.

Newman, Charles. *The Post-Modern Aura: The Act of Fiction in an Age of Inflation.* Evanston: Northwestern UP, 1985.

Nietzsche, Friedrich. *The Gay Science.* Tr. Walter Kaufmann. New York: Random, 1974.

————. "Truth and Falsity in an Ultramoral Sense." *The Philosophy of Nietzsche.* Ed. Geoffrey Clive. New York: NAL, 1965.

Norris, Christopher. *Deconstruction: Theory and Practice.* New York: Methuen, 1982.

Olderman, Raymond M. *Beyond the Waste Land: A Study of the American Novel in the Nineteen-Sixties.* New Haven: Yale UP, 1972.

Olsen, Lance. *Ellipse of Uncertainty: An Introduction to Postmodern Fantasy.* Westport: Greenwood, 1987.

Olson, Elder. *The Theory of Comedy.* Bloomington: Indiana UP, 1968.

Phillips, Elizabeth. "The Hocus-Pocus of *Lolita.*" *Literature and Psychology* 10 (1960): 97–101.

Piandello, Luigi. *On Humor.* Tr. Antonio Illiano and Daniel Testa. Chapel Hill: U North Carolina P, 1974.

Poggioli, Renato. *The Theory of the Avant-Garde.* Tr. Gerald Fitzgerald. Cambridge: Belknap P of Harvard UP, 1968.

Portoghesi, Paolo. *Postmodern: The Architecture of the Post-Industrial Society.* New York: Rizzoli, 1984.

Prescott, Orville. "Books of the Times." *New York Times* 18 August 1958: 17.

Reich, Walter. "The Enemies of Memory." *New Republic* 21 April 1982.

Robbe-Grillet, Alain. *For A New Novel: Essays on Fiction.* Trans. Richard Howard. New York: Grove, 1965.

Robertson, Mary F. "Hystery, Herstory, History: 'Imaging the Real' in Thomas's *The White Hotel.*" *Contemporary Literature* 24.4 (1984): 452–77.

Robinson, Fred Miller. *The Comedy of Language: Studies in Modern Comic Literature.* Amherst: U Massachusetts P, 1980.

Roth, Philip. "Writing American Fiction." *Commentary* 31.3 (1961): 223–33.

Rother, James. "Modernism and the Nonsense Style." *Contemporary Literature* 15 (1974): 187–202.

Rourke, Constance. *American Humor: A Study of the National Character.* New York: Harcourt, 1931.

Sartre, Jean-Paul. *Being and Nothingness: An Essay on Phenomenological Ontology.* Tr. Hazel E. Barnes. New York: Philosophical Library, 1956.

———. "Existentialism Is a Humanism." Tr. Philip Mairet. *Existentialism from Dostoevsky to Sartre.* Ed. Walter Kaufmann. New York: NAL, 1975.

Scholes, Robert. *Fabulation and Metafiction.* Urbana: U Illinois P, 1979.

Schopenhauer, Arthur. *The World as Will and Representation.* Tr. E. F. J. Payne. New York: Dover, 1966.

Schulz, Max F. *Black Humor: Fiction of the Sixties.* Athens: Ohio UP, 1973.

Scott, Nathan, Jr. *Negative Capability.* New Haven: Yale UP, 1969.

Selden, Raman. *A Reader's Guide to Contemporary Literary Theory.* Lexington: UP Kentucky, 1985.

Shute, J. P. "Nabokov and Freud: The Play of Power." *Modern Fiction Studies* 30.4 (1984): 637–50.

Simard, Rodney. *Postmodern Drama: Contemporary Playwrights in America and Britain.* Landham: UP America, 1984.

Simon, Richard Keller. *The Labyrinth of the Comic: Theory and Practice from Fielding to Freud.* Tallahassee: Florida State UP, 1985.

Skinner, B. F. *Beyond Freedom and Dignity.* New York: Knopf, 1971.

Smith, Fredrik N. "Beckett's Verbal Slapstick." *Modern Fiction Studies* 29.1 (1983): 43–55.

Smith, Willard. *The Nature of Comedy.* Boston: Gorham, 1930.

Sontag, Susan. *Against Interpretation and Other Essays.* New York: Farrar, 1966.

Spanos, William V. *Repetitions: Essays on the Postmodern Occasion.* Baton Rouge: Louisiana State UP, 1986.

Steiner, George. *Language and Silence: Essays on Language, Literature and the Inhuman.* New York: Atheneum, 1982.

Stendhal [Henri Beyle]. *The Red and the Black.* Trans. Lloyd C. Parks. New York: NAL, 1970.

Sterling, Bruce, ed. *Mirrorshades: The Cyberpunk Anthology.* New York: Arbor, 1986.

Stevick, Philip. *Alternative Pleasures: Postrealist Fiction and the Tradition.* Urbana: U Illinois P, 1981.

———, ed. *The Theory of the Novel.* New York: Free, 1967.

Sukenick, Ronald. *In Form: Digressions on the Art of Fiction.* Carbondale: Southern Illinois UP, 1985.

Sullivan, Jack. *Saturday Review* 7 July 1979.

Sully, James. *An Essay on Laughter: Its Form, Its Causes, Its Development, and Its Value.* London: Longmans, 1902.

Swabey, Marie. *Comic Laughter: A Philosophical Essay.* New Haven: Yale UP, 1961.

Sypher, Wylie. *Comedy.* Garden City: Doubleday, 1956.

Tanner, Tony. *City of Words: American Fiction, 1950–1970.* New York: Harper, 1971.

Taylor, Mark C. *Erring: A Postmodern A / Theology.* Chicago: U Chicago P, 1984.

Thiher, Allen. *Words in Reflection: Modern Language Theory and Postmodern Fiction.* Chicago: U Chicago P, 1984.

Tilton, John W. *Cosmic Satire in the Contemporary Novel.* Lewisburg: Bucknell UP, 1977.

Todorov, Tzvetan. *The Fantastic: A Structural Approach to a Literary Genre.* Trans. Richard Howard. Ithaca: Cornell UP, 1973.

Torrance, Robert M. *The Comic Hero.* Cambridge: Harvard UP, 1978.

Toulmin, Stephen. *The Return to Cosmology: Postmodern Science and the Theology of Nature.* Berkeley: U California P, 1982.

Trilling, Lionel. "The Last Lover." *Encounter* Oct. 1958: 9–19.

Ullmann, Stephen. *Language and Style.* New York: Barnes, 1964.

Vattimo, Gianni. *The End of Modernity.* Tr. Jon R. Snyder. Baltimore: Johns Hopkins UP, 1988.

Wallbridge, E. F. Rev. of *Lolita. Library Journal* Aug. 1958: 2183.

161

Wallis, Brian, ed. *Art after Modernism: Rethinking Representation.* Boston: Godine, 1984.

Walsh, James. *Laughter and Health.* New York: Appleton, 1928.

West, Paul. "Germany in the Aftermath of War." *Washington Post* 9 Nov. 1980.

Wilde, Alan. *Horizon of Assent: Modernism, Postmodernism, and the Ironic Imagination.* Baltimore: Johns Hopkins UP, 1981.

Willeford, William. *The Fool and His Scepter: A Study in Clowns and Jesters and Their Audience.* Evanston: Northwestern UP, 1969.

Wirth-Nesher, Hana. "The Ethics of Narration in D. M. Thomas's *The White Hotel.*" *Journal of Narrative Technique* 15.1 (1985): 15–27.

Wittgenstein, Ludwig. *The Blue and Brown Books.* Oxford: Blackwell, 1958.

———. *On Certainty.* Tr. Denis Paul and G. E. M. Anscombe. New York: Harper, 1969.

Zavarzadeh, Mas'ud. *The Mythopoeic Reality: The Postwar American Nonfiction Novel.* Urbana: U Illinois P, 1976.

Zuver, Dudley. *Salvation by Laughter: A Study of Religion and the Sense of Humor.* New York: Harper, 1933.

Index

167

Lance Olsen is an assistant professor of English at the University of Kentucky. He holds the M.F.A. degree from the University of Iowa and the M.A. and Ph.D. degrees from the University of Virginia. In addition to numerous articles and short fiction, Dr. Olsen's publications include *Ellipse of Uncertainty: An Introduction to Postmodern Fantasy*.

The manuscript was edited by Elizabeth Gratch. The book was designed by Mary Primeau. The typeface for the text is Times Roman. The display face is Times Roman and Avant Garde. The book is printed on 55-lb Glatfelter paper and is bound in Holliston B-grade Roxite cloth.

Manufactured in the United States of America.